Jant

November Mourning

A mother's journey to find comfort
and solace following the death of her son

*Blessings & prayers.
Please to be first
Mary Jane*

Mary Jane Cronin

"Inspired"
by D.L.

Donated to HVS
in Memory of
Lou (Louie) T. Langevin
1961-2016

Wiggle Bug Publishing   Largo, Florida

Copyright © 2008 Mary Jane Cronin

ISBN: 978-0-615-23978-1

Care has been taken to trace the ownership and obtain permission, if necessary, for excerpts from the words of others. If any errors have occurred, they will be corrected in subsequent printings provided notification is sent to the publisher.

This is a work of nonfiction based on the author's experience of losing her child.

For information about ordering additional books visit:

http://www.myspace.com/november_mourning
or write me at
griefgirl57@yahoo.com

Printed in the USA

Jeremy E. Cronin

This book is dedicated to my son, Jeremy, whose life was ended abruptly at the age of sixteen. Jeremy is now in heaven and I believe he is watching over all of us. I thank him for the time his brothers and I had with him and for the love he shared with all who knew him. I thank him for the experience of being his mom.

Losing Jeremy was, and will continue to be, devastating for me. His death has also inspired me, encouraged me, and taught me that, although you may not be able to avoid a traumatic loss in your life, you can survive it and make it through the fire.

It is also dedicated to my three living sons Jaime, Jesse, and Jonathan for loving me. For knowing although not always the best solution, my intentions, were always good, and were based on my eternal love for them. Thank you for understanding that my spending many hours completing the research and writing of this book helped me to heal.

I love you all

In Memory of Jeremy

Acknowledgements

To the many mothers and fathers who like me have suffered the loss of a child and to those who shared their sorrow, so others could learn and heal I thank you.

Writing this story has been a personal experience, but seeing it become a book has taken the help of many people. I wish to thank some of my friends at The Hospice of the Florida Suncoast including Robert Arnold, Jackie Goehring, Wendy Gorman, Karen Jones, Janet Judge, Carolyn Smith, Virginia Spencer, Sandy Sunter, and Gerald Flanagan. These wonderful people encouraged, instructed, proofread and supported my dream of making this book a reality.

Associates Trade Bindery Company and Xpedx Paper and Graphics Store both of St. Petersburg, Florida and the staff of Fed Ex Kinko's Office & Print #1765 Clearwater, Florida were all heaven sent. Thanks to their support and guidance, this novice writer has blossomed into an accomplished author and publisher.

Rachael and Vicki, my special friends, thank you. You were in my life when Jeremy died, and continued to always know when I need to be comforted.

Table of Contents

Part Three

Foreword

Having recently had the opportunity to review Mary Cronin's book, *November Mourning*, it can be noted that the content of this book is very heart-warming and truly expresses the feelings Mary had with the loss of a child. Mary not only portrays the death of her son, Jeremy, but it also reflects her true feelings toward her other children. It is not easy to understand how one must go on and continue to express love not only to other family members, but to all those who surround her.

Mary just had to write about this. This is the way she was able to grasp an understanding of why this happened. It is very difficult to deal with the loss of a child under any circumstances, but the murder of one's child is much more difficult to comprehend.

This book is truly recommended to be read by all those who have lost a child and members of their families.

Jimmy Johnson
Mayor of City of Seminole, FL

A Message from Mary

Nestled between the happy season of giving thanks and the day of receiving gifts and praising the Lord, is for me, a somber day. Longing for the opportunity to sing Happy Birthday to my son, I instead shed silent tears. Tears fall every year on that November day when rather than growing old, he will forever remain sixteen.

Losing my son to a bullet is a memory that will stay etched in my mind forever. Along with that painful image is a second more joyful one. This one is of him at age six, waving to me as he ran smiling down the soccer field. As those early days following his death turned into weeks and months of indescribable emptiness, I searched for a comforting place to put all of these memories.

A combination of the lack of knowledge I possessed at the time of Jeremy's death coupled with an inability to work through my own grief was the primary motivation to begin my research and writing this book.

Searching for meaning and logic in a situation that did not make sense, I felt alone and out of control of my emotions.

I wanted to find out what other parents had done to help them with their pain and grief.

As I read and researched about emotions felt by other parents, I discovered they experienced and felt much of what I had.

In finding this common bond with fellow bereaved parents, I was able to accept and begin to heal after the death of my son.

Born a twin in the late 50's to a mother and father who already had ten children, bonding and nurturing came secondary to seeing everyone was fed and had clothes to wear.

Less than a year after my birth, the State of New Jersey determined my parents could no longer care for this many children properly and we were placed in the foster care system. Undernourished and in poor health, my medical condition required that I be transferred to the local hospital for medical treatment.

Learning that, although my twin brother required additional care and must remain in the hospital, I was to be released shortly and was in need of foster care, one of the nurses talked to her family about us.

For three years following our discharges from the hospital we were both foster children to a member of her family. The foster care turned into adoption and we remained with that family until we were adults.

Growing up with my adoptive family, my basic needs were met. I will be forever grateful for the love and care they showed me and my brother.

Emotionally, however, I continued to feel alone in the world.

Marrying a man I thought I loved, I was eager to start the family I always wanted. The family that had been in all my dreams, a family that shared memories and spent time together having fun.

In eight years four sons were born and we looked forward to tables full of family laughing together during holiday meals.

As a young family we were short on funds but enjoyed each other's company. Watching movies or enjoying the music the boys made together, I felt I had finally become a part of the family of my dreams.

Jeremy's death caught all of us off guard and completely unprepared.

Traumatic death had not been a part of the forty years of my life prior to Jeremy's death. Both of my father's parents died peaceful deaths when they were in their eighties. Their funerals were comforting tributes to a fulfilling and happy life.

Never needing to discuss death with my parents or my own children before, I did not know what a "normal" reaction was, what was acceptable or expected behavior.

Mistakes in judgment and inappropriate grieving left me, my husband, and our three remaining boys unequipped to express our sorrow felt after Jeremy's death. Families faced with a member suffering with alcoholism often refer to themselves as having an "elephant in the room". This symbolism referred to us.

The problem is always there but no one talks about it. Although we were all affected by his death - and it was around us all the time, we never discussed it with each other.

The boys did not like seeing me sad. Not wanting to make me cry, they appeared brave and accepting of the loss of their brother.

We treated Jeremy's death like that elephant in the room. Rarely did we mention Jeremy in those first few months, but he was always on our minds.

Teenagers are comforted by their friends and share their sadness and sorrows together. I, however, suffered alone in my sadness. Adult friends were helpful in the beginning, but returned to their own lives and my husband was emotionally unable to provide comfort to me and deal with his own grief too.

Parents interviewed in the books and journals I read expressed this same concern. The emotional journey of personal grief can be so draining that people are often unable to give to one another.

Looking back now, I see that my personal grief left my children alone in their own sadness. There had to be a better way for parents and their families to get the support they needed.

I wanted to know that what I was feeling was normal, that I was not losing my mind. I wanted to learn how to help other moms avoid my mistakes. The desire to find those answers is what turned my completing a school project into this book.

I hope that as you read through these pages you are able to learn something new from my writings.

That you will be able to find comfort following an experience every parent fears will happen to her child.

The death of their child

Chapter One
An Introduction to the Pain

The Unthinkable has happened; you have just been told your child is dead. For a mother, the emotions surrounding the loss of a child are similar to those feelings felt by a young child on his first day at a new school. Although people may be nice to you, and want to help you get through the experience, you continue to feel alone and isolated.

Grief is traditionally defined as inward thoughts and feelings of someone who is experiencing a loss in their lives. This loss can be anything from the loss of a friendship, parent, or even a divorced spouse, but, in my opinion, nothing can surpass the emotions that engulf you following the loss of your child.

The natural order of life for most people begins when they marry, and begin raising a family.

Their children grow from infancy through the school years to begin dating themselves silently hoping they too, will find that one special person, marry, and begin to raise a family.

November Mourning

During the child-raising years, a parent watches over their infant as they sleep and learns the child's patterns for sleeping and eating.

Encouraging their infants to walk and talk and helping their school-aged child to learn, a parent must also encourage them to begin to interact with others and to begin the stages of separateness.

It is during this time, parents begin to see that their child, who will forever be emotionally connected to them, will also one day unfold his or her wings and fly.

Beginning on the day the child is born, parents worry that their child might get hurt, kidnapped, or killed, and they try to keep them safe.

No amount of education, nurturing, or parental love can reduce the powerlessness or feelings of helplessness as a mother watches her child in pain or experiencing an illness they have no control over.

During childhood, parents are given an opportunity to provide direction and give advice to their child. But even when these conversations take place, a parent can still feel immobile and fearful that their child will not follow the warnings, and instead, will use their own judgment.

An introduction to the pain

Previous generations of parents who have raised teenagers will confirm, no matter what you say to them, that they still have their own judgment and opinions to question what you say.

Using that sixteen-year-old teenager's judgment is why my son is in heaven today.

Grief over the loss of a child, like any loss, is a personal experience. Grief is a process of learning to live without someone you love and to learn instead, to live with the emptiness and deprivation. This is a time to begin to learn how to rejoin the real world and go on living in it differently. Searching for meaning in what has happened to their child, parents often wish they could undo this tragedy and long for " what might have been".

Regardless of their religious and cultural beliefs, a life has been taken and cannot be returned. Friends and family surrounding the grieving parent cannot comprehend the intensity of such a loss.

In a sense, part of them *has* died with the child.

The hopes and dreams of both the parent and child are gone forever. The loss of the future and the re-creation of themselves through the next generation is now gone.

November Mourning

Grieving family members are expected to mourn their loss, but are *supposed* to do it appropriately and within a certain length of time. American culture believes it is acceptable to cry, to sulk and withdraw from others, even to be angry, but only for an expected length of time. The mourning parent is then supposed to "pull themselves up by their bootstraps" and move on.

Following this acceptable time frame, they are to live again, return to work, tuck away their pain and agony, and dry away their tears.

But for many parents, the loss of a child means that a part of themselves has died as well. The future they planned will forever be changed. Recovery time following a loss is as personal as the relationship with the deceased was and cannot be predicted by others.

Even though each surviving parent must go through the experience his or her own way, there are stages or passages that everyone tends to encounter.

In the first stage, many experience denial or shock that this could happen to someone they love. Disbelief, to some extent, can last for days, weeks, or even months.

Some experts say this is the parent's mind protecting them from the intense emotional aftermath such a loss produces.

12

An introduction to the pain

Coping with Grief and Loss, a book written by Sandra and Owen Giddens, begins with a story of a woman who lived in a small village. One day, she went to the religious leader with a small bundle in her arms, pleading with him to bring her baby back to life.

The leaders looked at the woman compassionately and said she must first look into the eyes of the other villagers and locate someone who had not been touched with personal death. Wandering the village for days and nights she talked with people and heard their stories about their own losses.

Following the talks she returned to the leader and said she now understood that death touched everyone at one time or another and she was now able to bury her own child.

In trying to understand death, Giddens explained that cultures and religions throughout the ages have developed many diverse beliefs. One such belief is the spirit of the person goes up to heaven to be with God. Another belief is that the spirit takes on a new form on earth. Protestants believe that God is with a person in both life and death. Catholics see death as God's will and view the passing as a journey to eternal life. Many of the Eastern religions believe in the immortality of the soul. Finally, some people choose to believe there is nothing after death; that everything stops there and the person is gone forever.

November Mourning

Regardless of one's beliefs, the emotions felt following the death of a child are real and must be acknowledged.

Grief is not a disease, a disorder, or an illness, but an indication of your connectedness to another person.

Grief can make you feel like you are going crazy or losing control.

One minute you are fine and the next minute you are sobbing uncontrollably with no understandable explanation. Loss of sleep, loss of appetite, reoccurring painful thoughts, and crying are outward expressions of the inward pain grief is causing you.

Often a newly grieving parent will be forewarned by others, others who have been through such an ordeal and wish to talk of their own reactions and recoveries. Well-meaning parents, who say that current feelings and emotions will come in waves, cannot fully prepare you for your own private journey.

Following the death of a child there may be a time when you will seem fine and then suddenly something "bubbles up" when someone asks you about your child.

An introduction to the pain

Maybe you find a memento belonging to your child or hear one of their favorite songs and suddenly you are transported to a past time when your child was alive.

In the days and weeks following your loss, you may have feelings that you are back in control of yourself, only to fall into a deep depressive crying stage.

Counselors, friends, and family members are all anxious to see you feeling better and not hurting.
In an effort to ease your pain they may tell you "It will get easier with time".

Yes, it is often true, that the waves of sadness and helplessness become less intense, shorter, and less frequent with time. However, in answer to the question "Does it get easier with time?" I would have to say "I don't think so." Grief does not follow a timetable. Everyone suffers differently and your grief will be like no other. Grieving for some parents is a way to stay connected to their child.

Continuous grieving helps keep their memories alive and retains a place in the family for that child.

A parent's grief is endless, but the intensity does diminish in time – for a mother's body could not endure the intense emotions felt immediately following the death of their child.

November Mourning

It is during this period of transitions that a parent begins the journey of understanding and accepting their loss by putting their emotions and grief in a place with no rhyme or reason and filled with many unanswered questions.

Self-blame, guilt, and feelings of failure may follow the realization of the inability to answer the "Whys" of the situation.

Self-accusation and fear that, as a parent, they contributed in some way to the death is felt not only by mothers and fathers but often by surviving siblings, who wonder why it was not them, and wonder if they are safe.

There is no set pattern of emotions a mother goes through following such a loss.

Not only do behaviors differ from cultural and religious beliefs, but also within members of a family.

Each family member may cope in different ways depending on their own past experiences with death, their age, and their connection to the person.

Circumstances surrounding the death, and support they received from others with prior tragedies in their lives, now influence reaction responses.

An introduction to the pain

All behaviors are acceptable and understandable, from the mother who now is over-protective of her surviving children to the father who, suffering from low self-esteem and feelings of inadequacy, is unable to care for his surviving children or wife.

As the reality of the loss becomes apparent, the only true way to reach the other side of the pain and begin recovery, is to experience every emotion that you encounter. Crying is acceptable, and so is not crying. Anger and depression may take turns as you try to make sense of the loss and begin to accept that your child has died.

Parents find themselves angry with the child for dying. If the child was killed, they are angry with the child for putting himself or herself in such a dangerous position, and if the child committed suicide, they are angry with the child for not crying out for help.

Anger can be generated in many directions to deal with a mother's grief. It can travel inward towards themselves, to other family members, to surviving friends of their child, and to families who have not suffered such a loss.

No one fully recovers from the loss of a loved one, and although you find that one day you can begin to face and accept the death, you are permanently changed as a result of the experience.

November Mourning

Remembering a lasting moment with the loved one, a conversation, an event or even their personal beliefs can leave a lasting memory affecting survivors.

Parents wanting to create a memorial for their deceased child may plant a tree, build a shrine, or begin speaking engagements that focus on a facet of their child's death.

Following his death, I had plans of erecting a coffeehouse for the teenagers in my community in memory of Jeremy. Hours were spent on supply lists, completing forms, as well as deciding what activities would be offered to the teenagers.

In 1999 I enrolled in Springfield College to get my masters degree in community psychology. The program was an intensive eighteen-month program that included a final project focusing on a personal presentation of our own choosing and the impact the research had on us.

One day one of my professors asked me if I was looking forward to having the coffeehouse. Was I prepared for the long hours I would spend there away from my family? Did I have the financial and business sense to make it a success or had I thought of hiring others to work for me?

An introduction to the pain

These questions surprised me, but started me thinking about the real reason I was opening a coffeehouse.

It was to show the world how much I missed and loved my son.

As much as I did not want to agree with my professor, Henry, he was right. I didn't want to be away from my other children and I didn't really know how to run a coffeehouse.

Henry suggested that I look at <u>why</u> - why I wanted to open that coffeehouse in the first place. He suggested I begin to build a new project from those thoughts.

The dreams and plans of owning a coffeehouse had filled my hours of sadness and despair following the loss of Jeremy. Those hours had given me an outlet for my grief and helped me through those first two years following the loss when I was especially vulnerable. Now I had a new mission to keep me from focusing on my feelings.

In looking inward, I began to ask questions. Was my behavior similar to that of other parents who had lost children? Did it matter how long the children were with them on earth? Would my understanding of how others dealt with their personal pain give me understanding to my own pain?

November Mourning

I began to understand that I wanted to know the answers to these questions and this would be the foundation for my graduate project.

Clark Moustakas published *Heuristic Research* in 1990, a book that was based on a form of research he defined as "a meaning to discover or to find". The book spoke of an internal search to discover the nature and meaning of an experience. It is thought that once the information is understood, the reader can develop methods and procedures for further investigation and analysis.

During this journey of gathering knowledge by investigating other sources, the investigator is said to also find self-knowledge and self- understanding.

To me, this implied that if I obtained information from books, journals, websites and by speaking to parents, I could help myself learn and begin to heal.

I wondered if everyone who has lost someone they love through death, divorce, or one of those unexplained, unexpected tragedies of life, finds the pain is always the same. In dealing with this pain, we, as a society, have been conditioned to "accept it" in silence.

Grieving mothers and fathers often experience emotions including disbelief, shock, and a sense of numbness. Although these emotions are felt by most parents, many think they alone, are having them.

An introduction to the pain

Much to the dismay of this mother or father, their friends and family hope and encourage them to "snap out of it", but they know everyone must go through their own fire.

The only way to recover and get to the other side with oneself intact is to experience all the pain and anguish that such a horrendous experience causes. To suppress one's feelings will not make them go away, but may instead cause them to lay dormant until the person encounters another crisis.

To begin my journey of understanding my personal feelings, and those of others, I visited the local public library. I looked for books dealing with grief and loss and read many of them, including' *A Child Dies: A portrait of Family Grief* written by Joan Hagan Arnold and Penelope Buschman Gemma and *On Death and Dying* by Elizabeth Kubler-Ross.

In addition to the books, I read published journal articles surrounding the topic of death of children and a parent's way of expressing pain and dealing with their loss.

From my home computer, I looked on the internet and visited web sites that were devoted to death, grief, and the loss of children.

More sites are being created daily as mothers and fathers search for tangible ways to make their child immortal and not forgotten.

November Mourning

Some examples include: designing a shrine or memorial, simply creating a website or blog that lists their child's favorite things, and sometimes poems written in the child's memory. Interactive sites and blogs allow visitors to write personal remembrances of their time with the deceased child.

The writing of this book has been over nine years in the making.

There were times I have been able to write for hours, but there are times that even now, are intermingled with bouts of denial that he is really gone
. Even now, ten years since that terrible day, I find myself fighting to face the acceptance that he is gone and that I will never see him again.

The reality of the expense and time needed to construct such a place like the coffeehouse allowed me to re-think my motives.

In discovering what other parents had written and felt, I began to realize that I did not need to build a shrine for others to see the intensity of my love and loss for Jeremy.

Chapter Two

A little bit about Jeremy

I lost Jeremy in August of 1998, and yet it feels like it was just yesterday. Jeremy, my second child, was born on November 30, 1981 and, although a planned pregnancy, was a complete surprise. His older brother, Jaime, was born in January of 1980, and as a young naive mother, I grew up with the traditional understanding that you were supposed to only have two children.

The first born child would be a son to carry on the family name, and he would be followed by a daughter who would be pampered and dressed all in ruffles. At that time the "birthing babies" part would end and raising them would now become the priority. Four sons later I found out how wrong that "wives' tale" really was. The night before Jeremy's birth, my husband, who had selected our first son's name, told me to pick out a boy's name as well as a girl's name just in case we had a son.

I selected the name Jeremy

November Mourning

Jeremy came into this world singing and never stopped. Early years of his life included Jeremy singing along with his father who played guitar, and later with his brothers in harmonies that could melt your heart. Jeremy was in chorus beginning in grade school and while in high school, was included in an all-county chorus with special singing engagements at Disney World.

Friends were special to Jeremy and he would always have time to listen when one of them needed to talk. Blushing as the girls started noticing him as more than a friend, he remained true to one girl and spent hours on the telephone with her planning a future together.

I am pleased with the young man Jeremy had begun to develop into. His heart was full of love, he cared about his family and friends, and had hopes and dreams for his future.

Jeremy was eager to begin his life outside the city limits of Largo and took his GED when he turned sixteen years of age. Passing the test on his first attempt was the sign he needed to show him that he was on his way.

Listening to musical tapes he made before he died, singing alone and with his brothers, brought me comfort, as well as pain. Searching for ways to understand why a young man with so much to give to others, was taken from our lives so soon, I silently wept.

A little bit about Jeremy

During those first few weeks following Jeremy's death I must have heard numerous times from friends and family "How are you getting through such a horrible situation? I do not know if I could do it if I were you". On the outside I looked composed and in control of myself, but inward I was dying a little myself.

Comments such as those, made by well wishing friends, made me wonder how other parents have learned to deal with the loss. I wondered if they too had experienced the sense of helplessness surrounding their lives that I had following the death of my son. Thoughts and questions needing answers filled my head.

Jeremy's motto was to put his friend's needs ahead of his own and he was always available to listen any time they needed him.

On his birthday one year he asked his friends to please get him cards that showed how they felt, not presents that he knew they did not have money to buy. When he was alive he completed a paper for school about how he wanted his future to be. In the paper he said although he was from a large family, he only wanted two children. He said he wanted to be able to afford to get them everything they wanted, and to spend the individual time with each of them that having more kids would not allow.

November Mourning

Being a mother to three other boys, I then began to understand what Jeremy might have meant in his paper and what he went through as a sibling to three brothers.

I used a more collective type of behavior when it came to raising them. Following Jeremy's death, I have begun to spend more individual time with each of the boys.

I tell them I love them more often and try to do more things with them individually, like going to a movie or getting a bite to eat.

If I had known I would not have him forever,
I would have spent more time with him -
And, told him more often that I loved him.

I cannot be there for Jeremy any longer, but I can learn from his school paper and from his passing. I feel I have been a good mother to my boys. Through the difficult years including getting a divorce from their father, to my returning to work and continuing my education, I have always let them know they are my reason for being.

As a result of my loss, I began to play a more active and supportive role in my surviving children's lives.

A little bit about Jeremy

When we removed Jeremy's bed from his room, we found written in marker, behind his bed, on the wall: "The key to life is forgiveness". Shortly after his death, Jewel, who was one of his favorite singers, released a song entitled "Hands". The chorus sings out, "In the end, only kindness matters". Even now, whenever I hear the words to that song, they continue to have an emotional impact on my thoughts and actions.

I have begun to forgive Jeremy for being in the wrong place at the wrong time, for taking chances, for putting the family through this pain, and... for leaving me, and have begun to be grateful for the time he was in my life. But the waves of anger and moments of sadness - - will never be completely gone.

The Night Jeremy went to Heaven

The night began as most other nights in our household of four growing boys, with the older ones making plans to be out in the community with friends and the younger ones begging to go along. My oldest son Jaime was eighteen and planning to go out with his girlfriend later that night and was now watching television.

Jeremy asked if he could spend the night at his friend's house and could he take his younger brother, Jesse. I said he could go but his brother had to stay home. Maybe Jaime could take him over for a while and bring him home later that night. The teenager thrill of playing cards, drinking Mountain Dew, and talking about girls was my understanding of the plans for the night. I did not know until that evening that Jeremy had also been agreeing to take part in something that night which would result in my losing him forever.

Jeremy worked with a young man who was interested in buying some marijuana and asked my son if he knew where he could get some. Jeremy had met the young man three weeks earlier when he began working at the local KFC. He offered to make a few calls on the man's behalf.

A little bit about Jeremy

As I write these words years after losing him, feelings of guilt and disbelief rush over me that I was not aware of my son's drug experimentation, or the reasons for his indulging in such behavior.

The two boys made pager calls throughout the day to each other, but the young man made another call as well - a call to purchase a gun.

That night the friends gathered as usual to play a game of cards – spades was their favorite. Jaime had taken Jesse over and was now at the 7-11 convenience store next door calling his girlfriend to tell her what time he would be going over to her house. The young man had made arrangements with Jeremy to stop by the card game to make the switch of marijuana for cash.

Arriving with another younger boy, they talked for a few minutes, and the young man asked Jeremy to step outside for a minute.

Three minutes later our lives were changed forever.

November Mourning

Jaime heard the gunshot and ran to his brother. The young man hopped in the van he had arrived in and took off – the police and 911 were called – Jeremy was dying in his brother's arms. The other people playing cards did their best to keep Jesse, their younger brother inside and away from the scene that will be etched forever in Jaime's mind – the loss of his brother.

Being awakened from a sound sleep, my husband told me there had been an accident and we had to go the hospital right away.

Arranging a sitter for my youngest son, we went to the hospital – with no information.

Was it Jaime, Jeremy, or Jesse who needed me at that moment? Had there been a car accident? The police had said nothing.

The hospital staff could only say that Jeremy had been shot. They would do their best to save him. I went home to get my youngest son and brought him back to the hospital with me to wait.

The night was spent waiting...waiting at the hospital for answers and waiting at the sheriff's station while the boys were being questioned. As a mother, I needed to have all my boys with me to try to help them understand this situation - - one that made no sense to me.

A little bit about Jeremy

The staff at the hospital tried all they could, but he had been shot in the head, just below his right eye and it had traveled upward in his brain, and he was pronounced dead in the early hours of August 30, 1998.

Days of making decisions such as what to fix for dinner and where to go on the weekend were replaced now with decisions including whether cremation or a cemetery plot would be the best choice and what type of casket to send my baby to heaven in.

Jeremy loved the beach and would often drive down during storms to watch the rain and the waves rushing to and from the shore.

He also loved to sit outside our house at night under the street light with his friends just singing or talking about life now and when they would be older.

It seemed appropriate to select a cemetery plot that put him near the water, under a street light and right at the edge of the cemetery street so his friends could continue to visit him and talk at nights.

Friends, his brothers and I would often sit there alone, or together, sharing our daily events and voicing our sadness that Jeremy was not here to share them. Playing guitar and singing or quietly sitting alone, we mourned our loss.

November Mourning

In the surreal life that I walked in during those few weeks, I often "fooled" myself by saying he was at work or driving around with his friends. Believing that at any moment he would walk through the door and this would be just a bad nightmare.

Secretly hoping when I finished doing the laundry, and carrying his clean clothes to his room, he would still be in there, listening to music or talking on the telephone.

Many days had me playing a tug-of-war with myself in an effort to hold things together and be strong or to retreat into my own sadness and grief.

Days of appearing strong in an effort to help my husband and boys, kept me from not facing the reality of his death, and from dealing with my own inner pain and grief. Trying not to cry in front of the children, yet feeling like I had lost one of my limbs, forced a denial that lasted for months, until one day something happened ...and it hit me.

Jeremy was gone

Although I was able to purchase the casket and plot at the time of his death, the marker had to be purchased and paid for in installments. Selecting a green marble stone with the inscription mentioning him being a loving son, brother and friend, it also included the words "Go with a Song in your Heart".

A little bit about Jeremy

Music was very important to Jeremy. Singing with his brothers or with the radio gave him an outlet to show the emotions and feelings Jeremy held inside.

The day the marker was paid off I went to see it in the ground. A ground I had been visiting on a regular basis, a ground on which I laid flowers and spoke of loss, but a ground that was bare.

That day a gleaming, green marble marker told me the truth – that my son, Jeremy was indeed physically beneath the earth, and his soul had indeed gone through the gates of heaven.

This jolt of reality put me in fear for my other children's safety. I was afraid to leave them alone and afraid to let them leave the house.

I had been working the third shift as a supervisor, and I was now afraid that if I called, no one would answer. Fearing that they were not sleeping, but instead that something had happened to them, forced me to stop working.

I sent my other sons out with cell phones and encouraged them to go out with each other and not to put themselves in danger.

November Mourning

The family of six was now five and everything had changed. Each of the branches of the family tree has handled the situation differently.

My oldest son sought comfort in his friends and wrote songs in an effort to help with his loss for his brother. He appeared to have accepted the loss on the outside, but he shared later that it was a daily challenge to live without his brother.

His brother Jesse, who often played guitar, went to the cemetery with his stepfather often and they talked about their feelings. Jesse was unable to play guitar for a long time without being sad, but the pain slowly healed and he continues to be an accomplished musician.

My youngest son, who was only ten when Jeremy was shot, was placed on anti-depressant medication. What appeared to be a good thing at the time proved to be only an emotional bandage, and once the medication was stopped, the feelings were there in full force and now needing to be resolved.

A second doctor the emotions had subsided, and, although he had wanted to cry and feel pain, he was not able to while on the medication. Once the feelings surfaced, my son wrote letters to Jeremy and his grandfather, who was also in heaven, telling them to take care of each other.

A little bit about Jeremy

He took a tape that Jeremy had loaned him to the cemetery to allow Jeremy to listen to it in heaven and to help accept the fact that he was gone.

Jeremy left an impact on all that he came in contact with.

He was very charismatic and his personality and likableness helped him advance in employment quickly. Working at KFC he had already at age sixteen, become a candidate for assistant manager on his shift. Jeremy was one of three boys that were killed that year who attended the high school, and although he had left high school, and had earned his GED, he had made such an impact on his fellow classmates that they included him in the anti-violence rally memorial held at the school.

When a family suffers such a tragedy they can either band together to survive the loss or they can drift apart. Our family became separate sufferers as the reality of losing Jeremy filled our lives.

Each member of the family sought comfort for their own pain and regressed inside themselves to avoid the possible hurt of losing someone else they loved.

November Mourning

Comparing my reaction to the loss of my son to those around me, I often asked myself why I was so strong one minute and so completely filled with pain the next minute. I found the explanation in my readings. Everything from past experiences, to personality types and personal coping skills influence a person's ability to handle grief.

It was when I accepted the rollercoaster of emotions I was on, and let them come as they would, without trying to explain them, that I was able to learn how to get through a day without my son.

If a mother approached me with the question of how she will feel during her grieving period, I would say that she may feel every emotion from happiness to anger.
Happiness that she had time with her child and anger that she didn't know it would end, and that she was not going to have them around forever.

I would tell her that she will feel the denial that it has happened to her once safe home. That she may have thought it only happened to other people, in other towns or to families who don't love and protect each other...but it happens to all of us.

A little bit about Jeremy

It happens to families that wake up happy to be alive and have future plans. To towns where crime is not on the rise and it is safe to keep your car doors unlocked without fear of someone stealing it.

I would gently tell a grieving parent that the bargains she tries to play with God to take her life and bring back her child never will happen.

That the anger she feels that someone would do this to her baby, or that her child would put themselves in such a dangerous position, will subside in intensity, but will never fully go away.

I would assure her that the pain she feels inside will diminish, as the sad thoughts of her child slowly will be replaced with comforting thoughts of happy times.

I would tell her that it does become a comfort to know that when your time to go to heaven approaches, they will be waiting to tell you how much they missed you too and how glad they are that you are with them again.

November Mourning

The young man stood in court during the trial and said he had bought the gun for twenty-five dollars the morning of the shooting. His defense was that he was trying to trade the gun for the marijuana. That Jeremy had been looking for a gun!

Jeremy was so against violence that he had never had a fight with another person in sixteen years.

He wrote poetry and songs full of love for a special girl and his hopes for a family and a happy life.

The young man who killed my son was found the night of the shooting not far from his own home. He had stolen his mother's van, had pockets filled with cash and over two pounds of marijuana. His need for drugs and money had cost my son his life. How could I ever forgive him? I wanted him to die just like my son had.

When the trial finally came to pass, it was over a year since Jeremy had been killed. The young man, just 18 years old, who once had a head covered in dreadlocks, was now clean-shaven and bearing a cross.

A little bit about Jeremy

His mother was crying that her son did not deserve to die, that it would not bring my son back, and that he was "just confused" about things. How could I be a compassionate counselor and want a young man to die? I fought the feelings within me for months.

- The judge ordered him to twenty-one years in jail.
- He will be forty years old when he is released in 2018.
- I was angry. Why did he get to live when Jeremy died?

But then I saw his mother crying too. The death of Jeremy had changed two families forever. The young man was sentenced to 21 years in jail, with time served and good time that may be added, as well as being eligible for release after eighty-five percent of his time is served, he could be out in fifteen years.

- *Fifteen years for ending the life of a young man with a promising future.*
- *Fifteen years for tearing a family apart.*
- *Fifteen years for breaking the hearts of two families...mine and his.*

November Mourning

Would having him spending a lifetime in jail bring my son back? I know it would not, but the anger, the rage, the hurt, the sadness and the pain I felt that day told me that I didn't feel that was enough time.

The emotions I felt the moment the judge made her decision included anger and rage - - rage that this boy was going to live and my son was never coming back to me.

I looked across the courtroom at the mother, who would lose her son for what seemed like an eternity, and it was then that I felt her pain inside me.

The skies cried that day, as did two mothers in a courtroom. They cried for the lack of control they had in their lives, for the loss of their future, and for the loss of their sons.

Chapter Three

Learning to live without my son

Jeremy was murdered while I was employed at the Home Shopping Network and was attending Eckerd College. I was completing my internship with the Resource Center for Women and assisting in helping women who were returning to school or the workforce. Although I have wished many times a day for the past nine years that I did not lose my son, I felt fortunate that I was surrounded by a very caring and skilled staff. Those special people cradled me in their arms and hearts and allowed me the time to begin the healing process at my own pace.

Reverend Tom Brown was my clinical advisor at the Resource Center and during my internship with the center we spent many hours talking about Jeremy. Listening to him talk about Heaven, spirituality and the afterlife helped me work through my grief.

During our talks he normalized my feelings and said it was an understandable reaction for me to feel Jeremy's presence in the room.

November Mourning

He told me it has happened to others and it would not be uncommon for me to get signs or messages from him.

Skeptics would say that getting messages or signs from the "other side" are nothing but the griever's mind playing tricks on them. For me, it was a way to still feel connected to Jeremy as I attempted to make sense of his death, and in my mind, to find ways to forgive myself for not protecting my son.

I decided that I want to write down the times that I felt Jeremy was with me before the time span causes my mind to fade.

Letters and Journaling

Following the loss of a loved one, many people find comfort and support in numerous ways including counseling, putting together a scrapbook of pictures and memories, or like me, to being journaling. Following the loss of my son, I could be found sitting at the computer writing.

Alone with my thoughts and feelings I would journal about my emotions. Sometimes I would play Jeremy's favorite music and other times the quietness of the house would call me to preserve my loss in print.

Learning to live without my son

The days prior, during, and following Jeremy's memorial service and funeral were hard for me and continued for a long time afterwards to be a blur.

Not wanting to accept and deal with all the preparations regarding his death, I continue to be grateful to the many friends, co-workers and neighbors that came to help me survive. With each thank you card I mailed after the service, I included the following letter:

Dear Friends,
As an expectant mother, one often finds she is waiting for what seems like an eternal nine months for her child to be detached from her and begin their life as a separate human being. The next eighteen years are then spent wishing many times over for that special connected closeness again.

Watching them grow, you struggle with teaching them to walk and talk in the same time span as all the other new parents you know, with a silent hope that your child will do it first. You know in your heart that your child is special but you want the rest of the world to acknowledge the same sentiment.

November Mourning

My son, Jeremy, was a special young man and the world did know it, maybe even sooner than I did.

Then suddenly, in the early morning hours of August 30th, he was shot and killed, and in an instant taken from our lives forever.

Lost in the rules of the household, such as "Clean up your room" and "Are you sure you don't have homework?" I focused on teaching him responsibility and self-worth while the rest of the world was getting his heart.

He often talked for hours on the telephone or in the yard to his friends as they confided their joys and sorrows to him. They sought Jeremy's advice on what they should do about school, getting a job, or about a new love in their life, and he was always there to listen.

Agreeing to go into work, rather than enjoy his scheduled day off because the boss needed him, or going to the beach with a bunch of kids, his family, or even alone to simply hear the calmness of the sea and the melodic sound of the waves that most of us do not allow ourselves the privilege to enjoy was what Jeremy was all about.

Learning to live without my son

Feeling trapped in a body whose chronological age denied him of his dream of seeing what existed beyond the city limits of Largo, he began his task of overcoming those limitations. Taking his high school Equivalency test and passing it the first time at the age of sixteen, was just one of the many validations that the world couldn't hold him down.

Jeremy knew everyone's part of the production of "The Phantom of the Opera" and every song on Meatloaf's "Bat out of Hell" album. Music was his way to tell the world how he was feeling as melodies and lyrics (and the pounding bass) coming from his room often gave a clue to his brothers as to what kind of day he had.

Telling everyone of the plans he had to buy a van always began not with the kind of van it would be, or the year it was made, but about the elaborate description of the stereo system that was going to travel with him to see the world after he turned eighteen.

A famous person once said something like, "If you have three true friends in your whole life you are a lucky man."

November Mourning

Jeremy must have been the luckiest young man on earth.

Because of his multitude of friends who either worked or went to school, we decided it would be best to make his viewing from four o'clock until eight in the evening so they could come to pay their respects and wish him well on his trip to heaven. Little did I ever expect that over three hundred people would come to say goodbye to my son.

I took comfort in each young person, teacher or friend who approached me, recalling the memories they shared with Jeremy and their sorrow for my loss. Along with my family everyone present was also searching for a reason to hold on to.

Any reason that would explain why Jeremy was taken from us so soon.

Rarely does a person's memorial service fill a church as work, children, and the responsibilities of life keep us from going. The church was "bustin' at the seams" as Jeremy's soul was lifted up to the maker and all his earthly tasks were done.

Learning to live without my son

Only twice can the funeral home remember filling up all the roads of the cemetery as people left the church and continued on for the graveside service.

They did this for Jeremy...for my baby.

The people who attended his service allowed Jeremy to enter their hearts and will be forever changed for the difference he made in their lives. Looking around the room I remembered his motto on life: "If you can't be there for your friends, what good are you? That's what life is all about."

Jeremy showed what a true friend he was by the hundreds of friends who came to his farewell, and I want to thank all of you for your support to our family and my sympathy for your own sorrow.

May Jeremy's giving of himself to his friends and his determination to make something out of his life act as a motto for all of us as we fight the urge to give in to the grief and retreat into ourselves to overcome the loss felt by the sudden departure of someone we loved. Let us truly love our friends.

November Mourning

Journaling Letters

November 1998   Last night I was driving into the yard, I always scan the stations but come back to Star 95 because that was the one he loved. Asking for a song to talk to me (so I knew he was with me) I was hunting for the meaning of the last few lines of any song...in desperation to feel his presence.

The song "Push" from Matchbox 20 made me smile. I found that listening to Dave Matthews makes me sad and angry... he died wearing a Dave Shirt, but listening to Matchbox I often see Jeremy in that guy's eyes. As I sat there singing and crying I felt fullness in me as if someone was putting air into me if I were a balloon. I was only aware of the fullness not my body... the fullness was Jeremy with me.

He hugged me as only he can now, from the inside. After that song was over...without any interruption the new Jewel song, "Hands" came on. The first time I heard it was near the cemetery and I cried. It says "In the end only kindness matters...and was all ok in God's hands"!

Learning to live without my son

When we moved the bed in Jeremy's room, we found a writing that said, "In the end all that matters is forgiveness" He is telling me to forgive him for dying, he is telling me to look at the world differently...that forgiving and being kind to people is what life is all about! Not pushing for all that you want, or being to driven.

The first time I felt him was in his room...I got a far away feeling and then felt warmth.

It was like going into a trance in a way...the same thing happened last night. I was only aware of my eyes beating to the rhythm of my heart. In his room he came to me, and one night after I had driven home from college I was sitting in the living room and crying that I was missing him, and the warmth came over me!

I didn't want to move when it happens because I didn't want him to go away!

He tells me he is ok. "How many times did he say "It's ok mom, you go study, we're all doing fine. You have to do homework". Forever the comforter of the family, he continues to comfort me now.

I hope he doesn't leave me soon. It is all I have left of him.

November Mourning

<u>December 1998</u> Last night I spoke to the newspaper about Jeremy, it made it so real. I miss him so much.

He was such a big part of my life - he was just getting ready to take off with his life! I read about another boy in the paper who was killed - oh for a mother to go through such pain.

I don't know what to do - I walk around in circles I don't know what to do. I was thinking how I dismissed my father from my life, my whole family (both of them), how I dismissed my husband - it was hard, but I never went back to him. Sometimes it scares me that I have "dismissed" Jeremy so easily, and then other times I don't understand how I will ever get over losing him. The whole house seems so quiet.

Jaime is hardly here, if he is he is in his room with friends. Jesse is like Jaime, really non-sociable - not like Jeremy. Jeremy liked being with us - as much as he pretended to want to live alone; he was always around, by his choice.

I told the newspaper about how we as a family have suffered, how we are closer - more protective and fearful for the other boys. How hard it is for all of us not to shut down our feelings and not talk about it because it hurts too much.

Learning to live without my son

How Thanksgiving and Jeremy's birthday brought pain and tears. I talked about how we have no desire for Christmas - not knowing how does one go on?

It is now Saturday night and we have come home from the service. The paper did a nice article about us, Jeremy you would be proud. I don't understand nor ever will, but I miss you.

The service was nice - they read the names of people who died and were buried at Serenity Gardens. They sang a song in Hebrew and then a woman sang Ave Maria and I started to cry - as they had played it at your service at St. Patrick's Church. When it came time to sing Oh Holy Night, Frankie and Jaime were both crying.

Silently we all remembered the beautiful harmonies you and your brothers made when singing that song at church. Oh sweetheart - we miss you so. How do you get on - how do you live without crying?

Jeremy, you brought me 16 years of love! We had a few times that were bad, but we worked them out. I knew you loved me and so did your brothers - it is just so hard. It is like Jaime said - you think it will always happen to someone else - but it happened to us! I love you baby...

November Mourning

<u>June 1999</u>   The need to make this all real is what I fight. Between telling myself he isn't gone, and crying because he is gone, has left me drained. I wish I knew what to do, how to get along without you I feel like I have lost one of my arms or legs.

It was first mentioned by a psychotherapist, Nick, but also mentioned in a book I read, that after you suffer such a loss it is as if a part of yourself has been amputated.

I don't want to adjust to the change. I don't want him to be gone.

I just want to exist without him here, not admit that he is gone. I don't want to change the room; I just want to pretend that he isn't at home. Maybe he is at his friend Ian's house, maybe he is at work, maybe he's out "cruising for chicks"...but not that he is in heaven and not coming back to me!
I felt his presence the other night in the living room - it was a warm almost hot feeling of weight over me...I didn't want to move because he was there and I didn't want him to go away.

How can he always be with me and still enjoy the wonders of heaven?

Learning to live without my son

Is my inability to accept this keeping him from that? I want to so much be able to "get over it", to help Jonathan move into the room, to get past the hard pain...the numbness that follows me around...

I wish Jeremy had lived to give me a baby grandchild...it would have been a girl I am sure. He loved our foster child Katie, "bimp" so much. How I wish I had something tangible to hold and hug when the "miss you" gets too strong.

LETTERS TO HEAVEN

Jeremy,
I miss you so much. I feel sometimes if I could just go with you. I try to help everyone deal with your being gone...But no one seems to need me! Jaime has his friends - I don't know how he handled his holding you while you were dying. But he hasn't come to talk to me.

Jesse has Rachel. I am glad that she has finally seen the good in Jesse. He is so lost without your lead. But again, he still doesn't come to me.

Jonathan – who is ten going on twenty, seems to help me more than I help him. Out of everyone in the family he seems to have the best handle on his grief. He wrote a letter to you and told you he missed you. He then wrote a letter to grand pop and told him to take care of you. When I asked him if he wanted to talk about you he said he had dealt with it.

November Mourning

He still misses you, but knows you are in heaven. He said that although you are in heaven he talks to you whenever he "sees you" or feels your presence.

I have been able to have a few days in a row when I didn't cry.

Sometimes I feel guilty because I don't cry all the time. Although I am heartbroken, I have to be strong. Who will be if I am not the strong one? Sometimes I wish someone would be strong for me.

I miss you all the time. I do know if I join you in heaven, the family would be fine. They all talk to your step-dad and I don't even feel a part of the family anymore. Why can't he be supportive of my grief the way he is for your brothers?

I thought going back to school would be good - but if I were not doing everything- work-school-internship...I might be able to help your brothers....I might have to remember you are gone... Oh, Jeremy, It is like I am never here. I ran away from my grief and in doing that I don't know how anyone is doing...not even me.

Jeremy I miss you so much! I tried to empty your room during a moment when I was unable to cry. I don't know what to do...Do I try to move on or stay in the memories?

Learning to live without my son

I tried to do one thing to move on and people started telling me I shouldn't do it so soon. I made a video of your room before I packed everything up. None of it has left the house - it is just placed in tubs.

Part of me didn't want to do it, but Jonathan would have been disappointed.

He wanted a room of his own, and feeling a connection to you the way he does, I was glad it was going to be your room. I know...it cannot stay a dead room.

But what do I do when it is packed up and your presence is no longer there. How do I survive when you are really dead - - and not just out with your friends as I so often pretend. How do I empty you from my life? Why can't I come with you? The pain is so bad. This is too hard for me to do.

Research I collected during my own grieving showed that many parents feel the desire to join their departed child. Worrying that their child is frightened and alone, or as a mother, not being able to handle the intense sadness and grief, they are wishing to end their own life.

Many of these feelings and symptoms work themselves out in time, but if they are continuing or are unmanaged, the grieving person should seek professional guidance.

November Mourning

Dear Jeremy,

For someone who thought no one in the family cared about you... life has been a month-long nightmare since you left us. I can't go a day without hearing a song on the radio that you played so loudly.

God, the house seems so quiet now.

I had planned to hook your music in the living room, but I think Jesse should have your music. He was just coming into his own identity when you left. How much he felt a part of you as you let him into your world with Ian and playing cards and music. He still sees Ian at school sometimes, but Ian is now working with Robbie at U-Haul. Ian told us last week that Mia, his girlfriend, had a miscarriage last week - it really shook him up.

He isn't ready to be a daddy...but the fact that the baby was his, that was now gone... like you, really hit him hard.

We are all having such a hard time with you gone. At night when Jaime goes out with his friends and everyone else is in bed, I sit alone and just miss you.

No matter how hard we try - life is different since you died and putting our heart out again so soon is frightening.

Learning to live without my son

I know you understand why I can't go to the cemetery as often as your friends and brothers do...It is TOO hard ...it makes me too sad to be there ...and it puts me back to this debilitating reality.

One day on my way to the cemetery I went to the house where you died. Ian and his father no longer live there and the house was open.

I went inside.

The feel of the house was evil. I did not stay long, because I knew you were no longer there, but in Heaven. I rushed to the cemetery and fell to the ground next to your gravesite and wept.

You are no longer alive. You are not on a trip and will one day drive up to the house with stories of your travels.

You are really dead.

I fight so hard to forget. I have to play denial games - because I have to go on. I have to make money to keep things together as well as to keep the house and pay all the bills for your brothers.

November Mourning

Tomorrow I am going to meet with Serenity Gardens to discuss the plots next to you. Jonathan wants to be with you and so do I. I am assuming that Jaime and Jesse will be with their families so I have decided only to buy the two on each side of you.

Jonathan finds it better not to be home on weekends and often goes to his friend's house to sleep because being here makes it so real that you are gone.

For someone who wasn't home much with your working and hanging out with friends ...it sure is empty with you gone.

Jonathan has been seeing a counselor and is now talking about you. He tells me he fears going to school and being with people he does not know. Backpacks are not checked at school and he has dreams about someone pulling out a gun and shooting him.

Jesse has been talking to his girlfriend Rachel and friends about you and goes down to the cemetery at night. School has been real hard - but I told him you found that, even though you had passed the GED, you should have stayed in school. I love you Jeremy, I know you are with the angels and watching over us, but I wish you were still checking on all of us like you use to do at nights - just to make sure everyone was all right.

Learning to live without my son

Jeremy, I miss you...and I love you... I know you were a good person who was just in the wrong place at the wrong time.

I do fear that the "easy ways" of making money would have pulled you in and maybe got you in trouble...but I would rather have you here with trouble than to be writing you letters in my computer. Watch over me a little longer...Hospice should help me adjust to your leaving. I don't want to say they will help us get "over it"...because we never will.

My mom does not seem to understand what I am feeling. When my sister Sandy died at age 47, she never spoke of her sadness to me or anyone else.

She does not know how to reach out - and neither do I. But I want to understand. Friends of the griever also want to understand...they want to help...but they don't know what to say.

Good night my baby, say hi to Aunt Sandy and Grand Pop for me. Love mommy.

A reoccurring experience many grievers mentioned to me during my research was having a feeling the deceased person was in the room with them or they had been visited by that person in a dream.

November Mourning

The Dance

And now I'm glad I didn't know the way it all would end, the way it all would go.

Our lives are better left to chance I could have missed the pain, but I'd of had to miss the dance.

Holding you I held everything, for a moment wasn't I a king.

But if I'd only known how the king would fall Hey who's to say, you know I might have changed it all.

chorus
Yes, my life is better left to chance.

I could have missed the pain but I'd of had to miss the dance.

Sung by Garth Brooks Written by: Tony Arata

It has been a long difficult ten years without Jeremy, but I would never have traded the sixteen years I had with him in exchange for not having the pain.

Chapter Four

Trying to stay connected to a memory

Quietly lying in bed I would often ask God to watch over my son, and ask Jeremy to give me a sign he was all right in Heaven, alone and not scared. Through the darkness of the night I would often see bright lights in my head as my eyes stayed shut hoping - but not knowing what I was hoping for. Religion was not practiced in my home while I was growing up, and it was only after the boys were born that I attended church and began to read the Bible.

Prior to his death, although I always believed in a power greater than myself, I never had much need for God or religion. Alone in my room I wondered, what if I was not getting a sign from Heaven due to my years of not attending church. But one night it happened - Jeremy came to me in my dreams - - but it was nothing like I expected it to be.

November Mourning

There was a photograph taken of Jeremy at Busch Gardens, a theme park in Tampa, Florida. He had on a green knitted hat and was smiling for the camera. In my dream he came to me wearing a hat identical to the one in that photograph, but it was blue. He spoke to me and said he was fine - but it was different now. In my mind, the color change of the hat was signifying that change.

He smiled at me and I was no longer afraid, and then he was gone.

Following the night of my dream the songs on the radio seemed to change. The bands were still the ones he listened to, but the songs were newer ones. Although it seemed natural since they were releasing new songs after Jeremy died, to me it was saying "I'm still with you, mommy, it's just different."

After Jeremy's death there were many nights I was unable to sleep.

Saturday nights were spent in fearing that if I went to sleep, I would be awakened again with another telephone call from a policeman. I did not want to be awake at 2:00a.m. That quiet hour of the night when many people sleep in peace, except for me, represented a time of day when I had no control over the lives of the ones I loved.

Trying to stay connected to a memory

Visions of Jeremy and his brothers during that last hour of his life and the wee hours of that morning filled my mind both during my waking hours and in my dreams.

Newspaper Articles

The St. Petersburg Times, which is our local newspaper, published Jeremy's obituary along with an article about the shooting itself on August 31, 1998. On Dec 12, of that same year, they published a story about Serenity Gardens Memorial Park's annual memorial service and included my family's loss in that article.

Jeremy's was one of over 100 names read.

The service is offered each year during the holiday season to help families and friends who have lost loved ones cope during this often stressful and difficult time. The cemetery was lit with candles placed in bags with sand and distributed along the roads by the area boy scouts while the names of the deceased are read in the mausoleum.

During the interview I held onto a book of poems that Jeremy wrote along with pictures and memories of him boating in the Gulf.

November Mourning

As each boy spoke with the interviewer about their own loss I realized something important to our healing.

Being their mother who kissed their "boo-boos' and made them better, I had to now let each one of them deal with his absence in their own way

Shortly before the Christmas service The St. Petersburg Times published a follow-up article regarding our family and our loss. In the article they reported on an event designed to help the community heal. An assembly was held at Largo High School on Feb 20, 1999 where students, parents, teachers and community leaders came together to remember students who were killed.

Jeremy had been one of two boys who had been students at Largo High School at some point. Their deaths in the same year by brutal means spurred peers to look for ways to combat violence. Students and teachers at Largo High spoke, sang and acted in plays with the message of the plea to stop violence and turn it away from our homes, our families and our communities. About a dozen students formed the school's non-violence committee after learning of the deaths. The committee organized the event, during which the school gospel choir sang. One student read poems she had written and two others performed a dance routine to Sarah McLachlan's song *Angel*.

Trying to stay connected to a memory

The Home Shopping Network, a twenty-four hour mail order television show had provided me an opportunity to raise my boys and make extra money for eight years prior to Jeremy's death. Starting out as a part-time telemarketer in 1990, I was able to help my husband support the family. At the time of Jeremy's death I had recently been promoted to third shift supervisor and was in training.

During one of my trainings in a department, I was invited to join a dozen other employees in a training class with medium John Edward.

John Edward, at this time, had a television show called *Crossing Over.* The focus of the show was on him receiving messages from deceased people whose family members were in the audience.

HSN was selling a video that taught lay people how to be more receptive to those messages. The group entered a conference room where John Edward and his assistant were seated displaying the videos.

Providing us with answers to questions the people calling in may ask, my ears perked up. John Edward looked at me and asked if I had a question. I was slightly caught off guard by his request, but said yes. I explained that if I were a caller I would want to know if I would be able to talk to someone specific - not my neighbor's Aunt Mable.

November Mourning

Was that possible?

John Edward explained that the videos were to help the buyer become more "in-tuned"; but that the person could not just reach someone they loved who had passed away.

Completing the presentation, we were thanked for our time and asked to return to our working stations. I left the room and went to the bathroom with my eyes filled with tears. Realizing that people spent $200.00 or more for a visit with this gentleman, I composed myself as best I could and returned to the conference room. Telling him how I had lost my son recently, I asked if he could tell me if he was all right.

John Edward started telling me about Jeremy and his crossing over to the other side.

In just a few moments he told me who Jeremy was with on the other side, mentioning my sister who had died from cancer a few years prior to Jeremy's passing and both my father and father-in-law.

Mentioning their military connection he said one was a high ranking officer in the Navy and one was in the Air Force. He was right!

Trying to stay connected to a memory

Continuing to complete college, I would be turning 42 a month before my graduation from Eckerd College that May. John Edward told me he saw white flowers from Jeremy for my graduation without my mentioning this to him.

He said Jeremy wanted me to know he was all right and that his death was an accident. The final thing he said was Jeremy wanted me to know it was not my fault, and that I had been a good mom. Through my tears I thanked him for taking the special time for me.

Prior to my leaving Home Shopping Network, I attempted to leave my house and socialize with others. My fear of something happening to my children, or myself, kept me inside most of the time. I went to a dinner party at the home of a co-worker. While sitting on the couch next to a woman I did not know, we began talking. I mentioned that I was in college and did not want to be at HSN forever. She told me she saw me working for Hospice and helping others who had suffered a loss like my own. She offered to do a private reading for me at a later time. Intrigued, I allowed her to provide the reading with runes- a type of stone used to interpret a person's inner being.

November Mourning

She said many of the same things I had heard from John Edward and both times it brought me comfort. Trying to stay connected to Jeremy, over the years I visited other psychics and learned to read Tarot cards.

Many times over those first years I would scatter the cards and search the books for meanings - hoping to get a sign from Jeremy.

More times than not, the reading of the cards showed me in an empty life and being alone. Although I had three living children who needed me, I could not accept that one of my sons had died. I continued to search for ways to stay connected for fear that moving to a phase of acceptance would signify disloyalty and he would question my love.

Real or in my imagination?

For every person who believes in this type of connection, there are just as many who called me silly and wasting my time and money. Years of attending college counseling classes, I see that it really does not matter. Grief has to play itself out. Those songs, messages and dreams and my times of feeling his presence were and still are a comfort to me.

They made the unbearable a little bit more bearable.

Trying to stay connected to a memory

Reverend Brown, in addition to helping me cope with my own loss, also suggested I bring the boys to the Center for evaluation. He said the Center had counselors who could talk with them to assess their bereavement needs. My three remaining sons only visited the Center one time. The counselor's assessment indicated they were not in crisis and were not recommend for services.

One of the reasons that they may not have needed counseling at that time was because the Cronin boys were not new to loss.

When Jeremy was ten years old, a young couple asked if their four-month old daughter could join our family and be raised as a Cronin. After giving birth to four boys and doctor's orders to have no more Cesarean sections, I said yes to this young couple. Our family welcomed four month old Katie, affectionately known as "bimp" into our lives. For over a year the boys, my husband and I raised and grew to love her as we began the adoption process.

Katie's parents began to have second thoughts. After another year and a difficult court battle, Katie returned to her mother and our family had experienced its first loss.

November Mourning

The boys who were 12, 10, 8 and 4 at the time were devastated. Wondering how her parents could have just dropped a baby on our doorstep, and a year later come and take her from our lives, they began their own healing process. Jeremy slept with a baby blanket of hers for years and promised when she turned eighteen he would find her and tell her how much we loved her and missed her when she went away.

When we sent Jeremy to Heaven, along with the Mountain Dew, playing cards and letters from his friends, was that blanket that meant so much to him.

Married couples often struggle to stay together following the death of one of their children. Torn between needing to be supportive of each other, but often lost in their own grief, they separate and soon become another statistic of a dissolved union.

Two years after Katie was taken from their lives, the boy's father and I separated and later divorced. Seventeen years of marriage and four children could not hold together what the pain and sadness of losing Katie broke down. Visits with their father continued to be strained and the court soon ordered the visits supervised.

Trying to stay connected to a memory

Following Jeremy's death, his father and I had heated arguments on where to place the blame and guilt. Each of us felt behavior and actions of the other contributed to Jeremy's death.

Shortly after Jeremy's passing, his father left the United States never to see his children again.

The new millennium found the boys and me alone.

Doing my best to support, protect and guide them we often argued about my smothering them. Not having anyone else to talk to, I tried to hold on to them too tightly. Looking back now, I understand how they must have felt. But I was consumed with my fear of losing another child and the feelings of not having control to protect the people I loved.

Over the last nine years all three have left the nest and moved out, but like many parents know - they often return. As children, as well as young men we rarely discussed life without Jeremy. Prior to losing Jeremy, I did not have a loss in my life other than my father. My siblings and I miss him deeply, but being in his early eighties, he had lived a good life and did not suffer at his time of death.

Unprepared to openly share our grief we all grieved silently and alone.

November Mourning

Working for a hospice has educated me about children, adolescents and adult bereavement needs. Understanding that it may be easier to talk with a friend or engage in a physical activity while talking may be more productive than directly asking them if they are troubled. Many of my newfound techniques have helped the boys and me to understand our emotions and fears following Jeremy's death.

Music was Jeremy's way to express his heart and my connection with him after he died. Listening to musical tapes he made before he died, singing alone and with his brothers brought me comfort, as well as pain. Searching for ways to understand why a young man with so much to give to others, was taken from our lives so soon, I silently wept.

Jeremy's love for music did not end when he left our world and it is my belief that he communicated with me through songs on my car radio. Whenever I would visit the cemetery I would hear a song he loved either as I entered the gates or during my visit.

It became a ritual for me to shut the motor off and leave the radio running to "test" his presence, and he rarely let me down.

Trying to stay connected to a memory

Matchbox Twenty, Dave Matthews Band, Sarah McLaughlin's Angel or a Jewel song would radiate out of my speakers as I smiled to myself as I sang along and shed tears for my baby whose life ended far too soon.

Jeremy's father was a musician and music was played and sung from morning to night with all of the boys learning the guitar or violin.

Jeremy attempted to play the bass, but his true talent was singing.

I hold within my heart wonderful memories of the boys singing. Memories that include all the boys singing Christmas hymns at church and in Jaime's room while playing guitars and laughing together. Jaime my oldest son wrote a song for Jeremy as a way of working through his own grief. Jesse, who played violin and guitar since age 3 stopped playing music for over a year following Jeremy's death. He shared that he was too sad to play without his brother.

Jeremy started singing in grade school chorus and was one of a few hand-picked students from his school to participate in an all-county chorus for fifth graders. Middle school was the time for Jeremy to train and learn about singing. The school music teacher took special care with him as he absorbed everything he could. Following his death the school created a musical scholarship in his name.

November Mourning

One of their performances included songs from The Phantom of the Opera, Jeremy begged for tickets to the play. Dressed in his chorus tuxedo, he escorted a girl from the chorus to the Tampa Bay Performing Arts Center performance.

He asked for the soundtrack for his birthday that year. *Music of the Night* and a haunting song called *Think of Me;* filled the house for months, and were later played at Jeremy's viewing.

Jeremy and his brothers were followers of the Dave Matthew's Band since they began appearing in concert in the Tampa Bay area in 1994. They had all attended their concert a week before he died and he was wearing a shirt from the concert the night he was killed. A few years later the three boys bought me a ticket to attend one of their concerts with them. Rarely did I go with them to see performers with our taste in music being so diverse. But this was different.

Sitting with the boys at the concert and hearing the songs they all sang together; I felt Jeremy was with us. It seems only natural that Jeremy would speak to me through music. It was his life - it said what he couldn't. It helped him understand his emotions and gave him permission to feel.

Chapter Five

The Stages
of Grief

Years ago five stages of grief were introduced to help identify the feelings of bereaved people. Since that introduction of Elizabeth Kubler Ross's writings, researchers have dissected, questioned and added to these stages. Realizing now that they are not stepping stones that happen in chronological order, survivors now know they may weave from one stage to another. Survivors may also intertwine the stages for years working towards hope and acceptance. With a sudden traumatic loss such as murder, many feelings including fear, distrust, and anger have been discovered to be common among the survivors and have lasted longer and may return numerous times.

Believing these stages are valid gives many people a place to start working on their grief.

November Mourning

These words give the griever permission to realize these emotions are not only valid, but are shared by many others also struggling to understand life without someone they love.

Shock. This stage is often described by people as feeling completely numb. During my own grieving I found it hard to concentrate. Many thoughts filled my mind in the early hours of the morning following the news that Jeremy was dead.

"It could not be Jeremy; he was at his friend's house". "Maybe the doctor had made a mistake and he was not really dead"

Maybe it was not Jeremy and someone else had stolen his wallet" "How could this happen in a small city in Florida?" I can say now that I was in shock - for the first week, and many times afterwards, I would just float in a fog.

Being a diabetic it was important to keep my blood sugar levels balanced. Forgetting to eat, not having much of an appetite, or in an attempt to avoid my reality, sleeping too much, caused the levels to drop.

Denial. Denial is understandable. Just ask any person who has lost someone they love and experienced the intense emotional pain that followed.

The stages of grief

Physical, emotional, and psychological changes and a feeling of losing control can happen to the body and mind of someone experiencing grief.

Many people experience a temporary type of amnesia that gives the body an opportunity to, in time, accept the news and recharge from the emotional wearing down of the body their grief produces.

The danger of denial is that it can make moving on to healthier stages of life harder. Returning to work and focusing on my day-to-day tasks and continuing with college kept me in denial and allowed me to forget, even for a short time, that my life was forever changed.

I did not want to admit that my son was dead. So pretend I did. Telling myself Jeremy was at work or with a friend, kept me from facing reality and in my opinion, falling apart. "I did not want to cry in front of the boys, I needed to work, I had to be strong" were all things I told myself to keep it together. That lasted for a short while. Focusing on the trial and putting all my tears into the killer's criminal case kept me from facing the real fact, that Jeremy was dead.

Guilt. As Jeremy's mom, wasn't I the person who was suppose to keep him safe? The person he came to when he was having problems? Following his death I was consumed with guilt.

November Mourning

Questioning if my getting remarried or my returning to college was the reason he started using marijuana, and wondering, what I might have done to cause his death. Survivors often have thoughts that start with the phrase, "If only I." Moms are supposed to keep their children safe! They are supposed to know when they are in trouble. I had no clue!

The high schools are full of teenagers experimenting with drugs and alcohol, even in small towns like Largo, Florida. If only I knew he was using drugs. If only I had told him he could not go play cards that night.

If I held him closer, or been a better mother, were thoughts that haunted me for years. I know I did the best job of being a mother that I could at the time. Jeremy knew I loved him - for that I am sure.

I felt guilty that I wished the boy who killed my son would also die.

Being a counselor who helps people in trouble, I wrestled with emotions wishing justice to be served for my son and those of not wanting another mother, even Trevor's mother, to have to go through the intense anguish losing a child can bring.

The stages of grief

Anger. Anger is often present during the grief process as survivors blame others and themselves for their loss.

Anger surrounded of my dream of the perfect family and home.

I was angry at the boy who killed my son, angry at the doctors who were unable to save him, angry at myself for not knowing how to protect him...and Jeremy for dying.

Months turned into almost a year with our family trying to get justice for his death.

My anger turned into silent rage as I found myself wanting the killer dead.

Asking the judge to take the life of the boy who took my son's life caused many hours of me questioning my belief system and my career choice of a licensed mental health counselor.

Gone was the future of seeing Jeremy get married and give me grandchildren. Gone was the innocence that bad things don't happen to people I loved.

Gone was the feeling of being safe and thinking I could protect my children. Thinking I could protect them from the dangers of the world. I was angry that the boy who killed my son was allowed to live.

November Mourning

Bargaining and depression. Many days of those first few years were filled with me focusing only on my grief. Raised in a family where emotions were not openly expressed, I now found myself isolated and filled with feelings of loneliness.

Reality told me my son was dead, but I prayed to GOD asking for it to be a mistake. Saying if he were brought back to me I would go to church more often and be a better person.

Not wishing my other sons to suffer the loss of their brother, I offered my own life to the Lord.

Depression weaved itself into my life daily as we attempted to hold our family together. November and December brought Jeremy's birthday and many holidays that reminded us that our family was now broken and celebrations were better overlooked. After months of denial something happened that brought me back to reality.

Jeremy's marker for his grave was ready. Looking down at the green marble block the reality set in.

My sixteen year old son was really dead and my focus changed after that marker was placed at the gravesite.

The stages of grief

Fearing the death of a second child, I stopped working and stayed in the home. Fearing something would happen if I left them, or if I let the boys out of my sight.

After the marker was placed in the ground, I became withdrawn and fearful. Feeling the need to call the places they said they were going because I needed to know they had arrived, my paranoia got out of hand. My fears of something happening to them were also met with resistance.

The boys felt nothing would happen to them and thought I was over reacting.

One compromise I made was sending the boys out with my cell phone whenever they left the house. I often continued to call them when they went somewhere just to hear their voices and to ensure they were safe.

Hope. This stage of hope does not mean hope that your child will return or that things did not happen as they did. It is the hope that the survivor will return to the present with the promise for a brighter future. The hope that when someone asks about your child you can smile and remember a good time rather than swelling up with tears as you immediately go to that tragic day. There was a special day that when the songs came on the radio I sang along with a smile that he was thinking of me that day.

November Mourning

Acceptance. This is not a time when you no longer feel sadness. I loved Jeremy for sixteen years while he was on earth and will continue to love him and miss him until that day I join him in Heaven. Acceptance is adjusting to life without your loved one and rejoining the present.

My acceptance began to emerge the day I came face to face with Jeremy's marker at the cemetery.

Before that day I pretended that Jeremy was at work or visiting a friend. Pretended that every time the telephone rang it might be him saying he was doing fine. Visiting the cemetery made me face reality, but it was also a place I began to heal.

Jeremy E Cronin
Brother, Son and Friend
Go with a Song in your Heart
November 30 1981 - August 30 1998

Through my tears, sitting next to that marker, I asked Jeremy to let me move on. Realizing I could no longer continue my crying and grieving at the intense level I had been doing, I asked his permission to let me heal.

The stages of grief

I wanted him to understand my need to stop visiting the cemetery and to begin to be a mother again to his brothers.

Having my son murdered caused emotions and stages that normally may not be present in the grief process including fear, frustration and a sense of powerlessness over my world and the ones I love.

Prior to this tragedy happening, it was easy for me to believe I had control over my life and the lives of those people I loved.

Powerless to protect my children turned into fear as I did not want to let the boys out of my sight.

Fear that something would happen if I let them out of my sight caused me to take medical leave from work and rarely leave the house.

Coming home in the evenings I needed to check every room for safety to know no stranger was in my house.

Fearful of being alone, I tried to have someone in the home with me at all times, asking one of the boys to stay in and watch a movie rather than go out with friends.

November Mourning

Grief is a process...

- ♥ Grief must be allowed to happen.
- ♥ It is a natural human process of adjustment to loss. If it is not acknowledged at the time of the loss, it will remain within the person and will be expressed at a later time, sometimes years later.

- ♥ Grief cannot be bypassed, hurried or rushed. It always takes longer than one wishes it would.
- ♥ Attempting to shorten the process invariably leads to complications and extended pain.

Chapter Six
A book's look at
a parent's Loss

Beginning my quest to discover how other parents in the past had handled the loss of their child, I was overwhelmed at the immense amount of books for sale. Amazon.com offered 26,301 books under the topic of grief with almost 800 of them focusing on the death of a child. Written by proclaimed experts including psychologists, teachers, as well as parents, the writer offered to help the newly bereaved parent.

My local library was a great place for background material and I found numerous books dealing with grief and loss. Skimming through each one, I was able to select and checkout the ones that were more related to my personal loss. Although the choice was much slimmer than Amazon offered, I only had to swipe my library card to take the books home and read.

November Mourning

The first book to catch my eye was *A Child Dies: A portrait of family grief* was *written* by Joan Hagan Arnold and Penelope Buschman Gemma. The authors spoke with mothers and fathers who had lost children in diverse manners and of various ages. Reading each of these stories, I began to see how other men and women experienced the loss of someone they had loved.

Sitting in the library, surrounded by books filled with words that echoed my sorrow and sadness, I began to conduct my personal research.

What I found was that I was not alone. Reading the recollections of their loss and personal journeys, these stories written by both mothers and fathers had a similar element of sadness and despair. Whether their loss occurred recently, or fifty years ago, parents never seemed to have gotten "over" the loss, but instead learned to live in a life they knew to be uncertain and unpredictable - and without their child.

Recovering from the loss of a child, written by Kenneth Donnelly, included various excerpts from mothers and fathers who have lost children. One set of parents shared their story about losing their teenage son, Michael. They said it is important to remember adjusting to your loss does not indicate a reflection of being disloyal to your child's memory.

A book's look at a parent's loss

Knowing that you will never forget your child, the author suggests the bereaved parent try to remember the good things.

Angela, another mother mentioned in this book, described the first year following the death of their eight-year-old daughter as devastating. Angela's husband suggested to the reader that to get lost in the "Why Me" keeps a parent from focusing on the fact their child has died. The *why* doesn't matter, it is the fact that the child has died.

He also warned the fellow griever that people who appear to get well too soon are often really only putting a bandage on their wound.

Ruth lost her whole family in a car accident and felt the "sheer frustration" of not being able to control something so vital to parents - - the ability to protect their children. In time, Ruth began to realize that no amount of crying would bring them back.

Wishing for their return, desiring to race to their graves and pull them out, Ruth also knew she had to face the reality that she would never see them again. Ten years later, the sense of loss is still surrounding Ruth. She told the authors that the most difficult hurdle to overcome was the initial attempt to re-enter a world that can never be the same.

November Mourning

Elizabeth Kubler-Ross once stated that pain is necessary for growth and that people may even become stagnant without significant emotional events, without tragedy and without pain. Thinking of the time they will join their child and the family will once again be whole, the survivor often reflects on the memories they have of their child. Many mothers and fathers say they are different people as a result of their son or daughter's death. Following the loss of a child, a parent's priorities and values often change. Life is often viewed as more precious and has more meaning.

Beyond tears is a book that focuses on nine women who lost children. The mothers collaborated with writer, Ellen Mitchell to tell of their collective and individual journey of grief. The women had all lost children who were young adults at the time of their death. Jeremy was sixteen when he died and I found myself relating to many of the feelings they had experienced.

Recounting their individual journeys, similarities were present. Shock, numbness, and feeling as though they were functioning in a fog, filled their first year, as did mine.

A book's look at a parent's loss

The parents said the bonding they shared and having someone to talk with helped them with their loss. What would they say if they had one day with their child? Many of the mothers and fathers spoke about saying they loved their child, would apologize for not keeping them safe, and voiced regrets in their childrearing.

Their sentiments echoed many private conversations I had with Jeremy following his death.

Phil's story, as portrayed in Marguerite Bouvard's book, *Path through Grief: A Compassionate Guide* explains the circumstances surrounding his daughter's death.

In an instant, his life was forever changed when a driver, who was not paying attention to where he was going, killed his daughter. Seeing the man go to trial, only to return to drive again while his daughter was gone forever, caused him to relive that horrible day over and over again.

Questioning thoughts overflowed Phil's mind. Thoughts such as "What if he had done things differently that day, would his daughter still be here". Anger is an intense emotion and often fills the minds of parents who have lost a child to death. Anger can be directed at the person who caused the death or to the child themselves for this happening.

November Mourning

The murdering of a child, Bouvard explains, produces feelings of anger, disbelief, shock, and thoughts of being confused. Victims of a murder seem to be more obsessed in finding out even the smallest details as to the "whys".

These parents often replay the situation over in their minds, searching to understand the various emotions that now consume them.

For the bereaved parent whose child has died, rage is often now focused on the murderer and the desire for revenge.

Sorrow is felt for the loss of their loved one and anxiety about the security of the world cause the parent to look at life a little differently than before.

Survivors of a murder often find themselves having trouble sleeping or having their sleep full of nightmares. Feeling out of control of a once simplistic life, they are now filled with feelings of hopelessness and uncertainty.

When Jeremy's killer was found and arrested that night, our family innocently breathed a sigh of relief and thought justice would be served. An arrest does not always lead to prosecution and convictions. Unfortunately, convictions also do not always lead to stiff sentences or the full time being served.

A book's look at a parent's loss

What appears to be a clear case of murder may soon be found to be manslaughter, accidental death, or negligent homicide. These changes often reduce the required time spent incarcerated.

Murderers rarely seem to receive the sentence a victim's family feels is adequate. Court cases can take a long time to come to trial and a killer can be acquitted or receive lighter sentences than anticipated.

Living with Grief: After Sudden Loss: Suicide Homicide Accident Heart Attack a book edited by Kenneth Doka, Ph. D, included a chapter on sudden violent death. The book states that many survivors of violent deaths find their bereavement reactions are more intense than anticipated deaths and often last longer.

Focusing on criminal investigation and lengthy court battles, grief work and self care are often ignored. Emotions including anger, rage and guilt consume the grieved family member.

Reading this book I found myself being relieved in finding that questioning one's belief system, feeling fearful, and seeking isolation are quite common in cases such as mine.

November Mourning

Feelings of empathy filled my heart and head as I read the words of each of the mothers and fathers recounting their own loss. The thoughts and feelings described on the pages seem to echo my own experience, and I felt a connection to many of them.

Not surprisingly, I found myself sharing their pain.

Pretending that Jeremy was at work or a friend's home assisted me in my denial. Fooling myself into thinking, that if I didn't go into his room – and be pulled back into reality - that this would be just a bad dream. I related to the feelings of drifting away from reality to "a state of being foggy and disoriented". Being lost in the "Whys". Why did this happen to my son, to my family, and to me? This form of denial allowed me to not focus on the pain or the reality that my son was really dead.

The reality is that as parents, no matter how much we fight it, we really are helpless when it comes to another person's actions.

Be it the actions of a stranger, someone we know, or even those children we have given birth to.

A book's look at a parent's loss

What Helped Me When My Loved One Died, edited by Earl A. Grollman, is a collection of stories of personal loss offering various chapters recounting their losses including the loss of a parent, spouse, or a child.

The stories spoke to the reader of both sadness and hope as each vignette focused on what helped that person with their loss. The parents all mentioned getting support from friends, family, and community resources such as Compassionate Friends.

Compassionate Friends, just one of the agencies offering support to bereaved family members was started in 1968 by Reverend Simon Stephens. Two sets of parents whose children had died on the same day at the hospital took comfort in talking with each other. They asked the reverend to help them form an organization that would offer comfort and understanding to bereaved parents. To offer the kind of comfort and understanding that only someone who had lived through the same loss could provide. Compassionate Friends provides chapters throughout the world.

November Mourning

Florence Selder's cover stated she wanted to write a book that offered support to people experiencing a loss and to offer ways to get on with their lives in a positive way.

Finding that many of the current resources offered were technical and impersonal, she set out to interview over one-hundred people looking for commonalities and answers.

The book offers a collection of stories dealing with not only loss through death, it included stories about dementia, disability, employment, and divorce.

No matter what caused the loss, the emotions felt are often the same and the "recovery" is similar.

The goal of *Enduring Grief, True Stories of Personal Loss* was in my opinion, similar to my motivation in writing this book. Selder, through her research, found listening and talking about a loss, provided comfort and healing to the survivor.

She believed if the readers saw that other people experienced the same pain and despair they had, it would help their healing.

A book's look at a parent's loss

Catherine M. Sanders, a psychologist who specializes in bereavement wrote *How to Survive the Loss of a Child*. Rather than providing the reader with stories of bereaved parents, this book offers to "normalize" the grief process. Providing a commonality to the stages and steps of the journey, the reader can relate to the hope that they too will find a place of solace.

The bond between a mother and child is special and like no other. Sharing blood and body for nine months begins a life of hope, promise, and legacy no other can provide. In the book, Sanders speaks of the stigma the death of a child produces.

Friends shy away not wanting to talk or not knowing what to say. Alone, often with little support, the bereaved parent's recovery is often delayed and the journey filled with shock, anxiety, and withdrawal.

Acknowledging the pain and surrendering to your grief and pain is the only true way to begin to heal. Chapters on self care, including relaxation techniques and meditation, and giving the griever a "time out" from the pain, were beneficial to me.

The sections of the book promising the return of joy to the reader's life and encouraging them to learn to live again did not offer false hope or unrealistic outcomes.

November Mourning

In suggesting the reader practice forgiveness, acceptance, and have hope, the writer offers ways to ease their grief. While a parent may never get "over" the death of a child, but with these suggestions, guidance and in time, sometimes, one can learn to live differently in a world that will never be the same.

Celebrities may have more cash and fineries than the rest of us, but they grieve the loss of their children just as intensely as anyone else. Rather than many of us who grieve in the privacy of our own home and surroundings, their grief is in the spotlight with spectators watching their every move.

Writing about my experience has been a healing process for me and the completion of this book is an outward expression of hope to the rest of the world that recovery is not quick or easy, but possible.

The following celebrities have shared their sorrow with the rest of the world in song or books. Reading their words brought me a mixture of sadness and comfort that they too experienced the many emotions and heartaches I felt after losing a child.

A book's look at a parent's loss

Judy Collin's son committed suicide at age 33. Her recovery lead her to write a book "Sanity and Grace: A Journey of Suicide, Survival and Strength." and become active in suicide prevention for which she received the 2000 Survivor Award given by the *American Foundation for Suicide Prevention*. Judy Collins allowed her grief to be transformed into a ballad "Wings of Angels" for her son after his death.

In *Sanity and Grace*, Collins shared the events leading up to and following the death of her only child and her finding the strength to move forward. Collins like most grief-stricken parents strived to learn just to exist, and later to find solace in the face of grief and untimely loss.

Collins kept a personal journal for years prior to her son's death, but continuing to do so following his death helped her to get her feelings and ideas out.

Ms. Collins was quoted in an interview for NPR.com "I am always in favor of solutions, and I am also in favor of a group. I think, if you don't have a group, if you don't have a place where you can remonstrate, and discuss, and weep, and complain, and laugh -- you got to get a group".

November Mourning

Tony Dungy, former coach of the Tampa Bay Buccaneers and who is currently the coach for the Super Bowl Champions Indianapolis Colts lost a nineteen year old son to suicide in December 2005. In speaking about his son, Dungy said "He was a Christian and is now in heaven".

Quiet Strength' A Memoir was written by Tony Dungy and focuses on his faith and beliefs as well as talking about his son's death.

Dungy said the biggest regret in his life is that when he saw his son for the last time during the Thanksgiving holidays, he said did not hug him when he left, but only gave him a causal goodbye.

I felt that same way following Jeremy's death. If I had known that night that I would never see him alive again, I would have hugged him longer and told him how much I loved him.

A book's look at a parent's loss

Saving Graces, written by Elizabeth Edwards showed a private side of a public figure that, like many of us, faced a devastating tragedy.

In 1996 Elizabeth Edwards lost her son when he was 16 years old. Like my son Jeremy, her son Wade was full of hopes and dreams of a long future. In an instant a car accident took his life.

Saving Graces, a biographic book interweaves stories of her life including her discovery of cancer in her breast days before the presidential election of 2004 and her journey through the years following her son's death.

Reading through the pages of her book, I found myself nodding as she wrote of the feelings of emptiness she felt on that first birthday, Christmas and New Year's Eve following Wade's death.

Grieving the loss of her son, she also grieved the promise of his future. She, as I, would never see her son meet and fall in love, marry, or give her grandchildren.

November Mourning

Although surrounded by supportive people who wanted to help, Edwards turned to the internet for comfort. Like me she was drawn to other people in cyberspace who had experienced such a death. Searching for validation that what she was going through was normal, she shared her pain and tears.

She found that while she shared her own pain she was also providing comfort to strangers around the world with whom she now shared a common bond.

Edwards was able to make her vision a reality and the Wade Edwards Learning Lab, a computer lab built at the high school her son attended, was born.

I, too, spent many hours reading other mother's and father's stories about their loss. Following Jeremy's death I spent the next year designing and creating a coffeehouse for teens.

My own research showed that mothers and fathers share common emotions, feelings, and behaviors following the death of a child.

A book's look at a parent's loss

Sometimes life hurts us.

Sometimes it robs us of something, or someone, very dear.

Sometimes it causes us pain – a pain we did not choose and do not want.

Sometimes life severely restricts us.

When that happens, we feel out of control.

James E. Miller

November Mourning

A reoccurring experience many grievers mentioned to me during my research was having a feeling the deceased person was in the room with them or they had been visited by that person in a dream.

Chapter Seven
Visiting a Cyberspace Library

Being a college student at the time of my research, I was able to log into the Babson's on-line college library. Rather than focusing on books as a standard library does, this library focuses on published magazine and journal articles. Many journals were geared toward the general public and focused on self-help or human interest topics.

Ceramics Monthly's May 1997 issue offered a story showing a creative way for a mother to remember her child. *Healing touches: A Children's Memorial.* Written by Patty Rosenblatt spoke about clay pieces made by parents, siblings and friends for the children who died at the Dana-Farber Cancer Institute and Children's Hospital, Boston, The article spoke about a memorial service that was held in June of 1996 called "A Gathering to Remember". The service brought families, friends, and hospital caregivers together to honor children who had died of cancer.

November Mourning

Over 200 clay pieces of hearts, angels, stars, pet dogs, and baseball gloves made up the mural "Healing Touches" located in the entryway at the Dana-Farber Hospital. One mother recalled her child was a baseball player, so she made a baseball and glove with her clay.

People Weekly published an article on Sept 25, 1989 describing how a grieving mother turns the horror of Pan Am Flight 103 into a monument to her son. This woman's creation was a ring of eight sorrowing figures encircling a woman with one arm draped protectively over her womb and the other stretched heavenward in a gesture of despair.

The piece was dedicated to the mother's son who was one of 270 people killed when a bomb ripped apart Pan American Flight 103 over Lockerbie, Scotland. The sculpture represented her desire to have her child back and the anger felt from knowing he was murdered. She reported feeling "emptiness" inside her since his death.

In the months following the bombing, she discovered that working on her sculptures of her son helped to make him whole again in her mind. In her studio, she could pretend he was still alive.

Visiting a cyberspace library

When a Child Dies: How parents react to and cope with one of life's most devastating losses, by Ronald J. Knapp, was published in the July 1987 issue of *Psychology Today.* The article offered insight to many of the feelings and emotions numerous mothers and fathers interviewed felt.

Ronald J. Knapp stated in this article that the death of a child represents the loss of a future.

Relationships with each other as a family can change, and feelings they now have for each other and the living siblings of the deceased, may be different from those prior to the death. The parent may be faced with sorrow, sadness, and despair. Feelings can include: depression, anger, and bitterness, and if not addressed, can become long-lasting, debilitating, and more difficult to resolve.
Although everyone's grief is different, Knapp interviewed over 150 families who had lost a child and found significant similarities.

Many parents have a desire to never forget life with their child. They fear, as life continues on, they may forget the memories they have of their child.

November Mourning

I wrote many letters to Jeremy and often listed memories I had of him – now limited to being in my mind. Websites are created and trees are planted in an effort to share the child with the world and keep their memory alive.

Religious faith is revisited as parents search for answers and for comfort.

Many parents, who had not previously placed an importance on religion before their child's death, now sought meaning.

Mothers and fathers who had drifted away from their churches, agnostic parents, and parents who were unsure of the existence of an afterlife began looking for some insight.

Often because it was too discomforting and painful to accept the idea of their child being totally gone, they began to search their backgrounds for some evidence that death was not the finality they had once thought it to be. Following the death of his son, one of the fathers interviewed said he had once thought religion was a myth. Not sure if what he read was true, he felt the idea of an afterlife was now comforting at this time.

When Jeremy died it brought me comfort that he may be in Heaven with other family members who had gone before him.

Visiting a cyberspace library

All parents need to talk about their loss and what they remembered about their child.

This similarity was evident during my personal research. Many of the parents and loved ones who had experienced this same loss wrote books, created websites, or became leaders of support groups.

The foundation of this book began as a final project for my college degree in 2000.

There are parents who cannot bring themselves to discuss the death of a child for months and even years. Often it is because they are discouraged by fellow family members and friends who did not know how to talk to them. Some mothers and fathers said they felt they were a burden and did not think others wanted to listen to them talk of their loss.

Many parents wanted to follow their children to heaven

The loss of my child was so devastating for me that although I had other children, my desire to be with Jeremy was at times very strong. I feared he would be alone. That fear coupled with the wish to escape the magnitude of emotions the separation had caused me, I found myself at times filled with thoughts of suicide.

November Mourning

There is more of a focus on family

Many parents in the article found they were now turning toward shared family time with a new respect, looking at this time as one to be enjoyed and relished together.

I came to understand I could lose my other children in that same quick way I lost Jeremy - with them never knowing I loved them or how proud I was of them. Following his death, I changed my priorities and started spending more time with his brothers.

Shadow Grief can be felt by any survivor but is more prevalent with mothers and fathers who have lost a child. People face many losses in their lifetimes including girlfriends, boyfriends, and jobs.

Over time, many of these losses, which once produced traumatic reactions, tend to subside and life continues for the survivor. This cannot be said following the loss of a child.

Situations, memories, and current lifestyles are changed and affected by the loss of the child. Parents and their emotions following the loss of a child are changed forever.

Life will never be the same.

Visiting a cyberspace library

Over time the surviving parent will cry less often and find they are again able to talk about their child without breaking down, even though they know in their hearts they will never fully recover.

The Courage to Grieve author Judy Tatelbaum M.S.W., explains that grief feelings are harder to deal with than other feelings because of their intensity and the multiple emotions that are often involved. After the initial shock wears off, the flood of emotions including anger, guilt, and anxiety can be overwhelming and frightening, especially if the parent does not know that all of these reactions are normal.

Not expecting or understanding the emotions they are feeling, a grief stricken parent may begin to fear they are losing control. This fear of losing control and the attempt to suppress it can cause many parents to emotionally shut down.

Suppressing their emotions to avoid feeling them may be our current culture's answer, but feeling our emotions and dealing with the pain is crucial to moving forward through the grief process.

November Mourning

Prevention Magazine published *Beyond Grief: A Guide to Reconciling Life after Loss* written by Ardath Rodale and Sharon Stocker in their August 1994 issue. The authors of this article wanted the reader to know that experiencing grief over the death of a loved one is a natural process.

Although our current culture in America does not always allow people to express grief adequately, grieving people need a support system to help them work through their loss. It is through this open grieving that the survivor will eventually become reconciled to the new reality of their lives.

One setback to effective grieving is abandoning the traditions of the past. Once we were able to publicly share our grief, but we have evolved now into a society that grants less and less permission to express our sorrow and be supported by the community.

In some cultures and religions, the bereaved person is not supposed to do anything for a week or two, or even longer. They are encouraged not to worry about the mundane, daily responsibilities, but to embrace their sadness and loss.

In modern corporate settings, by contrast, employees are typically given just three days leave, even if it's their child, spouse, or close relative who died.

Visiting a cyberspace library

Employees are expected to go right back to work with the unrealistic expectation that they will return, able to function at 100 percent.

Currently, society places a priority on maintaining an image of strength and resilience in the face of hard times. In reality, what is needed at this time is permission to really let go and allow the feelings out.

The journal articles I read focused both on professionals offering suggestions and opinions regarding the parent's recovery from the death of their child and those of parents trying to make sense of a senseless act.

Knapp and Tatelbaum's articles focused on the commonalties of bereaved parents and provided suggestions for working through the grief.

Ceramics Monthly and People Weekly magazines provided opportunities for parents to display an outward expression of their grief in artistic ways.

Journaling or creating scrapbooks and making collages of remembrance have been found to aid mending.

November Mourning

"When a person is born, we rejoice, and when they are married, we jubilate, but when they die, we try to pretend that nothing happened."

Margaret Mead

Chapter Eight
Words from the
World Wide Web

The internet has become a place for individuals to put their feelings and ideas out to the rest of the world from the safety of their own home. Visiting the websites written by mothers, fathers, and those of on-line counseling services provided me with insight and understanding of the feelings of other who have lost a child. Even in 1999, when I began my research, the internet was full of websites written by and about parents who lost their children.

Focusing on websites that were devoted to death, grief, and the loss of children, I read stories and articles not only of despair, but of hope. Through their connections with others and the implementation of their sites, many of these parents came through their own fires. None of the parents who created websites came through the journey unscathed.

They did however, often arrive, at a place of acceptance and resolution and have continued their daily tasks of a life without their child.

November Mourning

New sites are being created daily as parents search for ways to make their child live forever in their hearts and minds.

Once limited to planting a tree or making a memorial photo, many people now own computers and are creating websites.

The websites I visited often listed the child's favorite things, accomplishments, and sometimes poems written in their memory.

The amount of information on the Internet was overwhelming, enormous, and amazing. On-line companies were quick to offer me my own web page to preserve Jeremy's memory with only a credit card number. The majority of the sites I visited gave me information, compassion, and hope.

Any search engine such as Google or Yahoo will produce web sites offering books and videos, counseling, agencies advertising for clients, and personal pages of people who have passed away. It may take time, but be patient and the sites may help you too with your grief.

Words from the world wide web

The first website I visited was MOMS: (parents of murdered sons and daughters) a site that was started by a mother who lost her son. I related to this mother's story and website because she too had lost a son to murder.

M.O.M.S, is a place for parents to communicate with each other, to provide some information about the grief process, and to provide information to links of other sites that may be helpful to you as were to me.

http://www.moms.memorial-of-love.net

GriefNet.org is an Internet community of people dealing with grief, death, and major loss. They have thirty-seven different e-mail groups and two web sites. Their online approach to grief support provides help to people working through loss and grief issues of all kinds. This site provides a safe environment for kids and their parents to find information and ask questions.

http://www.GriefNet.org

The MISS Foundation is for family members experiencing the death of a child. They offer to share in the pain and will walk with bereaved.

http://www.missfoundation.org

November Mourning

The home page of Empty Cradles explains they are for everyone who has ever lost a child. Like other sites it includes links to online grief resources and offers some advice about things that have helped others. Reminding the grieved mother that she does not have to go through the pain alone, the site offers a compassionate heart, a listening ear, or a strong shoulder to someone who would like to talk. A mother's heart never forgets.

http://www.empty-cradles.com

Alive Alone is an organization for the education and charitable purposes to benefit bereaved parents, whose only child or all children are deceased, by providing a self-help network and publications to promote communication and healing, to assist in resolving their grief, and reinvest their lives for a positive future.

http://www.alivealone.org

Angel fire is a site constructed by a bereaved mom and author. There's a place to post your 'angel' story as well as some information about her book.

http:// www.angelfire.com/or/angelhugs

Words from the world wide web

Bereaved Parents of the USA (BP/USA) is a national non-profit self-help group that offers support, understanding, compassion, and hope especially to the struggling to rebuild their lives after the death of their children, grandchildren, or siblings. BP/USA is open to everyone regardless of the age or the circumstances of the death. There are no dues or fees to become a member of BP/USA. All work on both the national and chapter level is done by volunteer bereaved parents with a strong desire to help other families survive the death of their children just as they were helped when their children died.

http://www.bereavedparentsusa.org

GROWW, is an independent haven for the bereaved developed by the bereaved. The pain from losing a loved one, whether spouse, child, parent, sibling, or friend can be the most severe suffering one ever endures. Such is the power of grief. It can take over your life and become the centerpiece pushing everything else to the side or to the back. The pain can be overpowering and consuming. GROWW is a place where peer groups in an online chat room environment teach that you have "permission to grieve".

November Mourning

The GROWW website tries to teach its visitors that what they are feeling is NORMAL. Everyone's grief is unique and everyone's grief is the same.

http://www.groww.org/index.htm

The mission of The Compassionate Friends is to assist families toward the positive resolution of grief following the death of a child of any age and to provide information to help others to be supportive. The Compassionate Friends is a national nonprofit, self-help support organization that offers friendship, understanding, and hope to bereaved parents, grandparents and siblings. There is no religious affiliation and there are no membership dues or fees. The secret of TCF's success is simple: As seasoned grievers reach out to the newly bereaved, energy that has been directed inward begins to flow outward and both grievers begin to heal.

http://www.compassionate friends.org

Words from the world wide web

HEALING HEARTS for Bereaved Parents is a website dedicated to providing grief support and services to parents who are suffering as the result of the death of their child or children. Having gone through the pain themselves, they have struggled with and worked on their grief and finally made peace with it. Their website offers the following links to other websites offering support.

http://www.healingheart.net

Guideline Publication is a site for parents who would like to acquire literature on how to explain death to their children.

http://www.Guidelinepub.com

This site is a grief referral directory only. It will provide you with complete contact information to find the products and services that will help you on your grief journey or, if you are a caregiver, to help you discover excellent support resources for all kinds of loss.

http://www.goodgriefresources.com

Support Systems

Support systems, which once have included family and church, are now often absent and alternate support may be hard to find. It has been shown that when people are allowed to grieve, they become reconciled to the changed world more quickly and are able to better accept the reality of the situation.

There is an old traditional saying that says "Time heals...", but it's also what you do with that time that is important. Perhaps the most important step to take in the grieving process is to allow time to heal and have the permission to grieve.

In some cultures and religions, the bereaved person is not supposed to do anything at all. Staying home for a week or more while everyone else brings you food and necessities allows the grieving person to begin to heal. This act of kindness helps in two ways: first, that there are people around for them to talk out their feelings with and second, by giving the griever freedom from having to worry about daily responsibilities

Words from the world wide web

The concept of confiding in a friend or supportive listener may sound like a good idea, but according to a newspaper article in the St Petersburg Times on June 25, 2006, only one in four Americans reported they had a true confidant.

At the time of death, many people are responsive to your pain, but as the weeks go by, more often than not, these well wishers begin to decline. Sometimes it is the everyday business of their own life, but often they withdraw because they don't know what to say or are afraid they may say the wrong thing.

Not knowing that just listening is the most important thing they can do, well-meaning friends and family members try to take the role of advice giver.

What helped me the most during those rough times was having someone listening to me talk out my feelings. What I did find out was that sometimes listening when they also were struggling with the loss was too difficult for them.

November Mourning

Finding listeners with whom to talk can be difficult. Friends often withdraw; filled with fear they may do or say something wrong. Some people, attempting to avoid the discomfort of not knowing what to say, take the role of advice giver. Thinking they have to have all the answers, they feel inadequate to help and stay away.

Grieving parents faced with this type of friend need to understand that it is not that your friends are unwilling to help. It's more that they feel clueless as to what to do.

You can't expect friends and family to automatically understand your personal fury when they're upset and trying to sort out their own emotions.

Support groups with survivors who have had a similar loss can provide the griever an avenue to express those feelings. Many groups serve specific grief situations, like the death of a child or a suicide.

Feeling like you are the only one with your emotions and feelings can slow down the healing process. To connect with others who share your loss and are able to validate your feelings while sharing in your sorrow can be very helpful to your recovery.

Chapter Nine
A Survey in the Making

The majority of the research found in the books, journal articles, and on the web suggested that there was a general progression of loss following the death of a child. I wanted to speak directly to other parents who have lost children to confirm whether they felt the way I do. To obtain the information and begin my research, I compiled a list of questions for the other parents. I then answered them myself and wrote my own personal story of loss to show I, too, was suffering from the death of a child.

I explained to the people I questioned that I was searching to find out how other parents were dealing with the loss of their children and only wished for bonding, comparison, and comfort in learning how to deal with my own loss.

I talked with other parents in person and through interactive web-sites about the problems women face when trying to overcome the pain of the loss of a child.

November Mourning

Together, we looked at the options for counseling and healing and came to a conclusion as to what we felt was the best course of action to assist the grieving mother.

Below is the questionnaire as well as the responses of the parents who answered. As expected, only a small percentage of the parents questioned, responded. Losing a child and dealing with the emotions that follow are hard to relive. I am grateful for the men and women who did respond.

A boy named Jeremy:

Jeremy was a bright sixteen-year-old boy born on November 30, 1981, and was anxious to begin life as an adult. Completing and passing all of his GED requirements, he was training to be an assistant manager at local KFC when he was killed. His love of music included performing with the All-State-Chorus while in school and making many tapes of him singing along with the radio or alone with his brothers playing the guitar.

In the wee hours of August 30th, 1998, I received a call that there had been an accident and we needed to go to the hospital. Jeremy had been shot and died at the hospital that night.

A survey in the making

I have found in looking back that I spent most of the first year bouncing around the first three stages of grief: denial, telling myself he was just not home at the time, anger at myself for not keeping him safe, at him for being in the wrong place at the wrong time, at the killer for thinking someone else's life was so expendable, and finally, bargaining.

I found myself bargaining that if Jeremy would just walk through the door I would behave differently, go to church more often, <u>anything</u> that would make this bad dream go away. Once his marker was put in the ground, reality hit me and so did depression. I left my job, cried often, and searched for a place to put this excruciating pain.

I have returned to college for my Masters degree in community psychology with the hope of helping others suffering, like myself and my family members have, since August 1998 when Jeremy joined God in Heaven. Without an extended family in Florida, we have been healing slowly, and it is through this questionnaire that I seek the stories of others who have lost their children, and the change, impact, and emotions this horrible experience has caused them.

It is not my intention to exploit your loss, for talking about it even two years later brings tears to my eyes. I only wish to understand and compare how other parents have dealt with losing their child.

November Mourning

Results

I received a 20 % response from the surveys I sent out to the parents on the internet who had also lost a child. The age of the children who had died ranged from being stillborn to over 21 years of age with the death occurring as early as 1989 and as late as 1998.

Elizabeth Kubler-Ross prepared a "guide" many years ago listing the feelings a person felt experiencing a loss in their lives. The list included denial, bargaining, depression, anger, and finally, acceptance. All of the parents who responded reported that they had gone through all five stages, but many suffered most with acceptance. Some reported that they continue to do so at the present time.

All responding mothers and fathers seem to have shared my feeling of helplessness and not having control over their lives. They were distraught about not being able to save their children. Many spoke about feelings of hopelessness at the thought of going on without one of their children. Family support following the loss of a child ranged from family being around constantly, to having only spousal support, or having no one to turn to during their grieving time.

A survey in the making

1. What type of grief counseling or outside support did you receive?

Parents said that online support system, a therapist for six-months, support groups for murdered children, Compassionate Friends, Hospice, and Church. One mother began her own online support group following her grief.

2. How has your family changed or dealt with the loss of your child?

Some mothers said she and her husband had become closer, more considerate of each other, and tried not to take anything for granted. Another mother said the opposite, and that they did not talk about their child and acted as if they only had ever had one child, when in fact, they had two.

3. What are you doing now to help recover from the loss of your child?

One mother said she and her family had planted roses for the last two and a half years on each holiday for their child, others planted trees in their memory, and some focused their energy on online support group. Parents, in trying to accept their loss, also said they had "turned it over to God".

4. *Where did you go for support?*

Hospice or Compassionate Friends worked for some. Others found comfort in their church. Websites and chat rooms provided support for a few. Most of them thought getting together in small groups and talking helped.

5. *How would you like your child remembered?*

Many of the parents surveyed including a mother who had suffered a miscarriage wanted their children to be remembered as being part of their family and forever be in their hearts. For others to know how: caring, loving, funny, a miracle, and very smart they were.

In 1999 and again in 2006 The Compassionate Friends (TCF) published findings from two surveys from parents who had lost at least one child to death. The estimation is that over thirty-five percent of adults have experienced the death of a child or sibling. They surveyed bereaved people to determine what helped them most during their time of grief in an effort to improve their services and raise public awareness.

A survey in the making

TCF randomly selected adults who had experienced the death of a child ranging from a young couple experiencing a still born death, to one where an eighty year old mother with a sixty year old son had watched her son lose his fight with cancer.

Over 80% of mothers and fathers surveyed said they received the most help from family and friends with co-workers and their church being their top three sources of support. Friends were listed by parents as least helpful, and in my opinion, may have been due to a lack of knowledge as to how they could help their friends during this traumatic time.

The second survey in 2006 asked the same questions and the response of friends, who were listed as a low support in 1999, became a primary support .Eighty percent of the surveyed people listed either friends or family as most supportive.

Nearly half of the parents said they were not aware of organizations in their area offering services such as The Compassionate Friends, hospice, or services through their local church.

With the introduction of websites designed by mothers and fathers began to surface and twenty percent of those questioned in 2006 found them helpful. Hospitals, doctors and funeral homes were listed as being non supportive in both surveys, but surprisingly, so were support groups.

November Mourning

Working parents surveyed said employers were sympathetic and understanding following the death of their child. Those parents benefiting from employer support expressed more loyalty and elevated work performance upon returning to work.

Working parents did suggest having more time off before returning to work or creating a flexible schedule were both indicated that if offered would be beneficial.

How did The Compassionate Friends survey compare to my on-line survey? Both groups of respondents felt family, friends, and their church community were the most helpful in their recovery.

I feel Jeremy's presence from time to time with the same warming sensation as I did that first year. Other times it is a "sign" like finding a penny in the driveway or somewhere I have been. Studies have shown many other survivors mention finding pennies and this often brings a feeling of peace to the bereaved person.

Personal Reflections

The results of my survey confirmed what many of the moms in the books and journal articles had shared. No one ever thinks so at the time - - but it does get easier.

♥ It can truly take at least two years to begin recovering from the loss.

♥ Support from friends, family or support groups lessen the recovery time.

♥ Participating in smaller groups of fellow survivors and frequent meetings were helpful in assisting parents who had lost a child.

The long journey I traveled to get to this place of acceptance and finding a way to live with Jeremy's death is over. No longer do I have the anger, fear, and depression that once filled my waking hours and dreams. No longer do I sob quietly on his birthday or anniversary of his death. Memories of the good times have gently taken over the frightening image of him lying in his brother's arms breathing his last breaths.

Does that mean I am over it?

November Mourning

I will never be "over" the fact that my son died before me. That he did not have the pleasure of loving someone special, or becoming the loving dad I know he would have been. I will forever be saddened that our once unified family, unable to comfort each other, crumbled and withdrew within, with each of us dying a little ourselves.

Having been through the loss of a child myself, I wanted to come to understand how other parents were feeling, and if they shared my emotions and range of confusion, rage, and pain. What I found in talking to mothers and fathers online was, YES, they had felt as I had felt.

I discovered parents who had also struggled with feelings of helplessness and who fought to remain in denial, because acceptance implied they had to go on living without their child. Although the range of reactions and responses differed with many of the parents, they all shared a common response. Many parents said they felt better when they were able to talk about their child's life and death. They also reported finding the support of other parents helpful in their recovery.

During my research and after compiling the results, I continued to go on-line to open chat-rooms of parents of children who had died from violence, from long illnesses, and infant death and continues to give me great comfort in difficult times.

What am I going to do with my results?

Reflections

One of the main phrases I heard at Springfield College was to "trust the process". My research for this book and own personal journey has taken me to places I never thought to go. I looked for opportunities to help others deal with their loss and pain and ended up working in a shelter for teens, a jail, and now with a hospice.

In the runaway shelter I spent hours listening to teenagers talk about the painful situations they had encountered in their young lives. Experiences that not even adults should have to endure. Providing Life Skill groups, I attempted to get the teens to talk about their losses.

Unbeknownst to me, children of this age group often have not come to terms with their emotions and in an attempt to exist in their current environment, must develop thick skins.

Working for Operation PAR, a substance abuse program for both children and adults, I was offered a position in the county jail helping adult women develop tools to remain drug free upon their release. Women as young as eighteen years old, hoping to get off drugs and return to a life of happiness and hope, agreed to enroll in the six-month in-jail program.

While working with these women I discovered a connection between their using drugs and their pain.

November Mourning

For some it was the goal of burying the pain that drove them to drugs. For others, it was using drugs that caused loss and pain to enter their lives. After talking with them I began to realize that maybe I could help others with their grief.

Working with a hospice for the last four years has provided me with a diverse loss experience. Before working there I did not know they help not only cancer patients, but people ranging from small children to the elderly. Hospice provides services for young people who once had plans and goals and families and children who never knew a life-threatening illness was going to come into their lives.

Helping others with their grief and to develop coping skills has helped me to become stronger. Whether it is a child, a parent or partner lost to death, I feel I am able to provide them with comfort, support and to assist them in finding a positive direction in which to put their pain. In helping others, I found that I have also helped myself. I feel I have found my purpose

As a parent searches for the "whys and what ifs" that could make this experience just a bad dream, they must perform all the formalities necessary to send their child to heaven.

I hope this book has shown other grieving parents that they too, will smile again, love again, and one day not be so afraid to give away their heart.

Reflections

One Sweet Day

Sorry I never told you
All I wanted to say
And now it's too late to hold you
'Cause you've flown away
So far away

Never had I imagined
Living without your smile
Feeling and knowing you hear me
It keeps me alive
Alive

[Chorus:]
And I know you're shining down on me from
heaven
Like so many friends we've lost along the way
And I know eventually we'll be together
One sweet day

Mariah Carey written with Boys II Men

I find comfort in believing Jeremy is smiling down on me and his brothers. That he is playing cards with my dad like I use to when I was little and having a family reunion with those who have gone before me.

What helped me with my grief?

Everyone who has lost a child whether the child was an infant or an adult will suffer the pain of this senseless act. I have included suggestions that helped me and others I interviewed to lessen their suffering. It is my wish that a few will help you to find comfort and peace.

Take Care of Yourself

Remembering to eat and get enough rest was a challenge. Being diabetic and yet not having a desire to eat caused me to feel lightheaded and sluggish. I had to be careful of alcohol, drug and antidepressant consumption.

Although my family and friends had good intentions no one really knows how to help someone else. Did I need a few moments of complete quiet or need to be with others who missed him and felt sad too? If you are fortunate enough to have a loving caregiver, tell that person to help you to remember to eat, sleep, and not overdo anything that can be taxing to an already emotionally and physically depleted person.

Reflections

The first few days are the hardest. Simple bodily functions are no longer second nature. It felt like I now had to learn to do daily activities all over again. Learn how to eat, sleep, dream, or even love someone. My heart was in shock and bruised.

You may not even remember how to care for yourself or for anyone else. All of these have to be learned again. In essence, you begin to reinvent yourself. Reinvent yourself in a life without your child.

When you start to feel your sanity slip, do whatever positive thing you can think of to hold on: pray, meditate, go to a spa and get a full body massage. When able to take a trip to a new place, stare at sunsets or starlit sky, lie in an open field and make shapes out of the clouds as they drift.

Do something for you! And don't feel guilty about it.

You can't do anything for others if you don't take care of yourself first. You can't love others if you don't love yourself first.

We cannot give from an empty well.

November Mourning

When you begin to feel better and feel a sense of renewal, think about extending the love you still want to express for your child in a way that will benefit others.

Take it Slowly

Losing Jeremy was like losing a part of my own self. The road back to a life not focused on his death took time. I had to begin slowly. Getting up, taking a shower and getting dressed was the first step. Fighting the urge to stay in my bed and be sad, I had to remember, remember that I had other children who needed me.

Finding a balance between accepting the companionship of my family and friends and allowing me the time for solitude and reflection was important.

During the next few weeks my emotions resembled the waves of highs and lows, emotions that many of the grief books warned about.

One minute would be spent feeling like I would soon fall apart, and another minute would find me filled with feelings of guilt. Guilt that I was now coping, that I was not crying for the loss of my son.

Reflections

In an effort to pretend I was doing fine, I did not grieve. At that time I did not understand that to hold in such pain can be harmful to a grieving person's physical, emotional, and spiritual well-being. Going through the fire and experiencing the pain is the only way to recover from the loss.

Suppressing your feelings or holding the emotions inside will only delay the grief. Do not rush your grief, be gentle, and remember that you loved this person for a long time. Accepting the loss and finding a way to live without them may take just as long.

Keep Yourself Busy

Find something to do to keep yourself busy so that you aren't so caught up in that cycle of loneliness and despair. I completely lost all interest in doing all of my favorite things: watching movies, playing on the computer and writing. How in the world could I take pleasure in day to day pastimes when my son was no longer alive?

So, instead, I focused on cleaning house, doing laundry and going back to work. In other words, I tried to stay busy and not think about it.

November Mourning

Try to occupy your time and mind with something that will make you feel useful. Focusing my attention on the needs of my family helped me get along.

In the first couple of weeks, we planted trees in honor of my son. Our local community park offers residents the opportunity to place a plaque under a tree in the park in memory of a loved one and we picked a tree we thought Jeremy would like.

The boys and I selected a tree that divided its branches. The tree was divided with three limbs and another with one limb going alone. Located just outside of the Community Center where many concerts are held reminded us that music will always be a part of Jeremy's life. Feeling this tree suggested the path of Jeremy to go to heaven alone and the three boys remaining on earth. The purchase brought us comfort and we all visited the tree often. A friend suggested I make a collage of photos. I poured over family albums for weeks selecting pictures of Jeremy and his brothers in happier times.

Picking out just the right pictures of my sons that were especially important for immortalizing into the frame took me weeks to finish.

Reflections

When I think about having done all these things in my son's honor, I know that I was trying to show the world that my son was still alive in me and in my heart, and that I could never use the past tense of the word, "love," in referring to him.

Keep a Journal

Turn your grief and the loss of your child into something positive. Keep a journal. This will help to sort out emotions and may turn a negative experience into a positive growth experience.

One consistent aspect in a successful recovery from one's grief was that parents needed to continue talking about their child. Recounting and reliving both the good or bad things the child did or said by talking to others, or journaling, can help. Encouraging this type of conversation, parents can begin to come to terms with the different relationship they are now beginning to build with the child who is gone.

The death of one's child is not the usual course of nature in a person's lifetime. This kind of grief is by far, one of the most difficult ones to cope with, and the most painful. Even if you don't feel that you're a good writer, journaling can be healing for you and may bring you comfort. Recounting memories of your life with your child may be difficult.

November Mourning

Tears and moments of sadness may erupt as you relive countless moments of joy in your past that are precious and priceless. Talking about these memories and reminiscing with others or in a journal or computer allows the survivor to hold onto the good events in our child's life while learning how to accept the devastating event that took their life.

Composing letters to Jeremy and writing about my loss, I was often filled with anger and blame. The intensity of my pain and attempting to not feel it often caused me to put off even typing the words.

There were times I did not want to even think about his death - - It was too hard.

Tears and sounds of sobbing came out of me while creating the personal pages of this book. For years I was unable to edit the text out of fear of those intense early emotions returning again. Feelings I had fought so hard to restrain were again coming to the surface.

At the time of his death and for over a year I wrote to Jeremy often telling him of the disbelief of his death, the frustration of the court case and how things had changed in our family and community since his departure to heaven.

Reflections

The acknowledgement of this pain is what evolved in me beginning writing this book. In time I began to realize that I actually felt better after my emotion- filled writing sessions were over.

They gave me permission to openly grieve. Surviving all of the emotions and turmoil that filled those first few years, I realized that my pain was lessoning. In being on the other side of my fire – my sadness-that was filled with the forceful sentiment of losing a child, I now understand. Understand that a mother must go all the way through that fire - experience her grief - with the same intensity in which she loved her child. Journaling helped me do that.

Give Yourself Permission to Grieve

Going through my pain, I needed to give myself permission to grieve. Grieve regardless of what other people needed or expected. Fearing my children would see me weeping caused me to harness my tears. Denying my grief may have sent the wrong message to my children - that showing sadness was wrong. Going back to work after only a few days may have been perceived that I was accepting the death and doing well.

November Mourning

The times I spent alone in my bedroom while the boys were with friends were spent crying, writing, and watching mindless TV. When the boys appeared to be adjusting much faster than I was, I began to realized that a person's grief is theirs alone – unique.

Other people can't fathom your pain.

In an effort to help or be sympathetic they may be over zealous in their efforts or they may pretend that you're being melodramatic and encourage you to "get over it". Set aside special times to cry and be "lost in your memories". Accept emotions "bubbling up" and tears coming at unexpected times and places. Find a special friend you can call when you are experiencing moments of sadness.

Recognizing Special Days

Over the years, it has helped me to begin anticipating and planning activities for those special days. Days I knew would be more emotional. Birthdays of my son, his brothers and my own, brought up bittersweet and painful memories.

The pain you feel is a reflection of the great love you continue to have for your child.

Don't do anything you are not ready to do.

Reflections

Jeremy died in August with his birthday falling on Thanksgiving weekend three short months later. Setting a place at the table for him – feeling guilty if I didn't, we were all consumed in sadness and shortly ended the meal. Birthdays included me baking a traditional cake for him and visiting his gravesite alone. Our family chose to take their pain inward, and the cakes often went untouched and we all cried alone.

Even now, nine years later, the anniversary of his death found me tearful and needing to talk about the young man I gave birth to who was now in heaven. Surrounded by comforting co-workers at hospice, I was able to share my stories of his life and death. Hugging me, they allowed me to share my grief and in doing so brought me comfort.

There are times I find myself caught unaware by a song, a gesture, or a voice that sounds like his and I fall to pieces.

I have said many times since his death that "Jeremy forever changed my life when he entered it and forever changed my life when he left it".

I spent over sixteen years loving him deeply- how could those feelings change just because I can no longer hug him good night.

November Mourning

Give of Yourself and Help Others Who Hurt

Once you are ready, there are positive ways to share what you have learned following your loss. However, there are other impulsive negative ways that do not help you or others and can, in fact, cause more sadness than gratification and comfort. Volunteering and giving of your time can be rewarding for some people. Sometimes the best way to cope with sorrow is to console another.

The challenge is to find your true fit.

During the first few years following Jeremy's death, I taught court ordered parenting classes to couples at the Resource Center and worked in a youth shelter.

We provided an eight-week program that offered parents new techniques that could reduced anger and assisted in reducing drug or alcohol use in their child.

Counseling teenagers at the safe shelter, I began to realize that my intentions of taking this position were not as clear to me as once thought.

Leaving the youth safe shelter I became employed with Operation PAR, a substance abuse prevention and treatment agency. My first assignment was to work as a community liaison that assisted parents in getting help for their children.

Reflections

Both of these positions were designed to help children who were already a challenge to their parents.

I understand now, that in an effort to "correct my own parenting mistakes", I was trying to prevent the behavior from happening. Thinking I was unable to "save" these teenagers and help them with their losses, I thought I could possibly help adults see the error of their ways.

I stopped working with adolescents to begin counseling substance abused women who were incarcerated. Counseling these women, I found many of them had begun using substances following a loss in their lives.

Many years of being under the influence of alcohol or drugs had caused them to experience numerous deaths of friends as well as family members in which they never addressed their losses.

With permission from Operation PAR staff and the jail administration, I created and designed a grief awareness curriculum.

Providing artistic and expressive outlets each woman would talk about her losses and how she had coped or not coped with the loss.

November Mourning

Many of the women had lost custody of their children due to their addictions and never talked openly to anyone about their emotions surrounding this happening.

Having your own agenda when it comes to helping others is a guaranteed path for failure. I understand now that, although my intentions may have been good, my actions were somewhat selfish.

I tried to help the mothers and fathers at the center raise children who would not misbehave and die like my son. I tried to get the children at the shelter to be compliant and talk about how sad they were because my own sons would not talk to me.

Group sessions in the jail were often spent telling the women that if my son had not been using marijuana he would not have been in the situation that killed him. Watching the women graduate from the six-month program, only to return following a relapse, caused me to question my credibility, intentions and job choice.

Shortly after his death I applied to The Hospice of the Florida Suncoast for a job as a counselor. When they told me it was too soon after his death to work with family members facing loss, I was crushed. In retrospect, they were right.

Reflections

Six years after Jeremy's death I was in fact hired by The Hospice of the Florida Suncoast. During those six years I was able to return to school and get my Masters Degree in Community Psychology. The degree provided me with the education and knowledge I needed as a counselor to facilitate both individual and group sessions.

It was my desire to help people who, like me, had experienced or were currently experiencing a loss.

Providing counseling and bereavement care to patients and family members admitted to the hospice programs has given me a sense of accomplishment. I am able to provide comfort to family members and patients who are questioning why they or their loved one, who has had a good life, would now be inflicted with a cancer or another life threatening illness.

The Hospice of the Florida Suncoast provides continuing education for their employees and I have learned new skills to enable me to assist in counseling offer services. In working with survivors I am able to assure them that the pain, which may never go away, will becomes less intense.

November Mourning

Many of us who have lost a child wish we had that magic wand belonging to Cinderella's fairy godmother. Without hesitation, our first request would be to bring our child safely back to us.

But, atlas, we don't have a rewind button or that special magic wand and we must learn to live everyday with a little piece of our heart broken.

The following suggestions have been gathered over the years and used to help ease the pain of many parents in your same shoes.

It is my hope that some of the suggestions will help you as well.

Reflections

Memories

♥ Carry or wear something that reminds you of the one who died

♥ Create a memory book or collage

♥ Recall and record your dreams

♥ Ask for a copy of the memorial service

♥ Plant something living as a memorial

♥ Light a candle of remembrance

♥ Journal to yourself or the person who died

♥ Listen to music

♥ Do something to help someone else

♥ Write about your experience

November Mourning

Recognize what has been Lost

- Consider the different types of losses you may have experienced in your life and know that it is OK to be feeling whatever you are regarding these losses.

- Try not to ignore or deny a loss which means something to you. Remember that it is <u>your</u> loss and that your loss is important.

- Accept and express the grief feelings you have.

- We sometimes think or say "I shouldn't feel this way". Everyone will experience their grief in a different, personal way and there are no rights or wrongs.

- Therefore, be accepting of what you feel and give yourself permission to express those feelings.

- Gradually, you can develop ways of adapting to your changed situation.

Reflections

Current and previous life experiences can affect our healing journey

Previous losses in your life

♥ Did you experience any deaths while growing up or before this death?

♥ What was your relationship to the other people?

♥ What was your age at the time of their death?

♥ What were the circumstances surrounding those deaths

♥ How did the death affect you and how did you respond to it?

♥ Did you receive support from others or suppress your grief?

Previous family reactions to death

♥ What were your family's attitudes surrounding death and their ways of expressing them.

♥ Was your family religious or did they talk about their grief and have traditions or rituals surrounding death?

November Mourning

Dealing with the Recovery of Grief

- Some mothers and fathers of children who have died, such as those whose child died following a serious illness are often more prepared for the loss. Although saddened, they are able to accept the reality of the loss sooner than others.

- The bereaved parent is unable to begin their recovery until they are able to accept the death. And experience the intensity of their feelings.

- The hardest part of grief recovery is giving yourself permission to see the person who died as a part of your physical past and accept new ways of thinking.

- A parent will never "get over" the loss of a child, but recovery has begun when the bereaved parent is able to re-enter life with a new identity and ability to enjoy life again.

Reflections

What does Grief feel like?

Grief can feel like many things. Just after a death has occurred it is very common for you to feel numb, as if you were in shock. This is how your body instinctively reacts to pain

You may find yourself searching for your child

- This form of searching may range from dreams that seem as real as life, all the way to hallucinations caused by familiar sounds, smells, and sights.

- These may come when you least expect them, causing you to be caught off-guard and unprepared.

- This searching is normal, and is an important part of adjusting to your loss. The griever may begin calling out to the loved person/thing and often asking for them to return.

November Mourning

Behaviors you may feel

• You may find you are eating too much or too little.

• Many people begin declining invitations and seem to have loss of interest in the world.

• Dreams of the deceased can be traditional dreams or nightmares.

• To avoid the reality of the death some people begin putting away everything that reminded them of their loved one - or get rid of everything too soon after the loss.

• Restlessness and not being able to stay at home alone is often felt. Many people begin driving around to find relief.

• Carrying objects and visiting places that remind us of the loss may bring comfort.

• Wearing clothing belonging to the deceased person or having something to hold that was theirs often reduces the intense sadness.

Reflections

Is it Fact or Fiction?

Fiction: The younger the child - the less intense your pain should be.

Fact: The reality is that the love of a parent is not contingent upon the amount of time we had with our child. Love simply cannot be measured in time. Would it have been easier to bury your child one year later? No. There is no easier time, no lesser pain. It is horrible whenever it happens.

Fiction: It has been six months - you should be over this by now.

Fact: You will never "be over" this pain. The pain never completely leaves. I will grieve my entire lifetime for Jeremy - he should be with me. The death of a child, at any age and from any circumstance, is a life changing event that will never be forgotten. You may however, learn some skills to assist you in dealing with the pain. Day to day life will never be "normal" again and you may never feel the way it used to - but time does help to ease the pain.

November Mourning

Fiction: Sleeping pills, antidepressants or alcohol will help to get you through this pain.

Fact: Some parents take pills or use alcohol after the death of their child, but eventually realize that they may have been postponing the inevitable. Grief is physically exhausting and mentally draining. Accept and embrace the intensity of your grief as a normal reaction to the most difficult experience a human could experience.

Fiction: You should have another baby.

Fact: Your deceased child's life is worthy of all the pain you feel. While another child will fill your empty, aching arms, it will never replace your other child. Instead, allow yourself time to grieve for your child who died. Do not rush yourself. Be cautious not to venture into an unprepared pregnancy too soon after the death of your beloved child.

Fiction: You will soon become yourself again.

Fact: Your child's death has changed many things about you and you will need time and patience to reacquaint yourself with the new person you have become.

Reflections

Fiction Support groups are for weak people.

Fact: The death of a child is the most isolating and lonely event a mother can face. Many grieving parents say that friends become strangers and strangers become friends. How can anyone else possibly understand the depth of this pain if they have never experienced it before? This is why support groups help. Support groups are a safe haven for parents to share the deepest of their pain with others who have experienced the same feelings.

Fiction: It is best to avoid discussing the loss

Fact: The bereaved need and want to talk about their loss, including the smallest details connected to it. Grief shared is grief diminished. Each time a griever talks about the loss, a layer of pain is shed.

Fiction: I am going crazy.

Fact: The emotions a mother feels following a child's death can be overwhelming. It can be frightening. Our usual routine suddenly annoys us and we feel out of place - even with our closest family and friends. Some parents are unable to perform at work, while others may become completely absorbed in their jobs as an attempt to escape the pain. It is a roller coaster ride.

November Mourning

Please Let Me Share My Tears

As a child if I fell and skinned my knee I would cry – and someone would comfort me. Sitting in a movie theater with a date, the tears fell openly as the actors playing a role convinced us that it was real, and someone would comfort me.

Why is it now, when my whole world had crumbled by the death of my child, do I feel it wrong to cry.
Fighting to be strong and keeping it together I hold it all inside. Tears are not a bad sign you know- for they are nature's way of helping us to heal.

They relieve the stress of my sadness.

When I fight back my tears I am trying to protect your feelings of helplessness and the awkwardness suddenly in the room. Once I allow my tears to come and go, I feel lighter for it helps relieve my pain. Talking to someone who is truly listening to me allows me to say aloud what I have been holding in for so long... That I loved my child and will always miss him

Alone in my room or with someone I trust, my tears flow often right now. Releasing my anger and denial, I know that one day the happy memories will appear more often than the sad ones, and my tears will lessen, and one day dry.

Reflections

How do you continue to live when one of your children dies? How do you enjoy the simple things like laughing at a joke or crying at a sad song, knowing that they will never hear the words? The thousands of times I have closed my eyes and begged for a chance to hold him again, to hear his "I love you mom"

The endless times I have felt he was with me, only to turn and find nothing but a rustle of a tree or a fleeing shadow. As a mother who held a newborn to her breast and wished them everything they wanted in life- the answers don't come easy.

Was it his time to return to heaven, and he now watches over me as I watched over him for 16 years? Was it a cruel fact of that fictional saying "being in the wrong place at the wrong time"? Did the devil win him over God with the two of them playing a hand of cards?

Never will I forget the smile, the pride of his moustache growing in, and the joy he got out of being a "babe magnet". I don't want to stop hurting!

Telling me I have to move on, to think of my other children - and myself...to not weep for the memories... what if I don't want to. What if I don't want to get over it!

My baby is gone...he is dead! And a part of my heart and soul went to heaven with him.

11-6-98

November Mourning

The night is dark and I feel so alone.
Only one of the six limbs of my family has been broken off the tree, but one branch missing affects the way the tree looks, and the health of the remaining branches.

How do I get past the pain? How do I accept that my baby is gone? What did I do to make God take my son? Why did he have to leave us all before his time was done?

I have read book after book of people who have suffered sorrow, in an attempt to find an answer that would tell me what to do. There is no road map to tell you how to feel and when it will end.

The remaining branches don't seem as close to the tree, and all have gotten older in their years and in their minds. Death makes you grow up fast, as you realize it could have been you.

What if another branch gets caught in a storm? Gets too close to a fire? Gets chopped down for firewood? How do I keep the other branches close and safe? When all they seem to want to do is bend and drift away towards the sun? Life is not like the comedies that are on television.

The real world holds heartache and tears and the parents of today cry as life takes away their children- making their worst fears a reality.

Reflections

Reference Bibliography

Arnold, Joan Hagan and Gemma, Penelope Buschman (1994) A Child Dies: A Portrait of Family Grief. Philadelphia: The   Charles Press Publishers.

Bouvard, Marguerite and Evelyn Gladu (1998). The Path Through Grief: A compassionate guide. Amherst, New York: Prometheus   Books. Amherst, New York: Prometheus Books.

Doka, Kenneth (1996) Living with Grief after Sudden Loss. The Hospice Foundation of America.

Donnelly, Katherine Fair (1982). Recovering from the loss of a child. New York: Macmillan Publishing Co.

Giddens, Sandra and Owen Giddens. (2000) Coping with grief   and loss. New York: The Rosen Publishing group.

Geollman, Earl, A. (1981) (editor) What Helped Me - When My Loved One Died. Boston: Beacon Press

Kubler-Ross, Elizabeth (1969). On Death and Dying. New York: Collier Books

Mitchell, Ellen, Barkin, Carol, et al. (2004) Beyond Tears New York: St Martin's Press

Moustakas Clark (1990) Heuristic Research. Design, methodology, and applications.   Thousand Oaks, CA: Sage Publications, Inc

November Mourning

Sanders. Catherine M. (1992) How to Survive the Loss of a Child. Filling the Emptiness and Rebuilding Your Life. New York: Prima Publishing

Selder, Florence, Kachoyeanos, Mary & Gissler, Mary. (editor) (1997) Enduring grief: True stories of personal loss. Philadelphia: The Charles Press, Publishers, Inc.

Grogan David, A Grieving Mother Turns the Horror of Pan Am Flight 103 into a Monument to Her Son. People Weekly, Sept 25, 1989 v32 n13 p44

Klass Dennis The Deceased Child in the Psychic and Social Worlds of Bereaved Parents during the Resolution of Grief. Death Studies, March-April 1997 v21p147

Knapp Ronald J. When a Child Dies: How parents react to and cope with one of life's most devastating losses. Psychology Today, July 1987 v21 p60

Rodale Ardath and Stocker Sharon. Beyond Grief: a guide to reconciling life after loss. Prevention, August 1994 v46 n8 p88

Rosenblatt, Patty, Healing Touches: A children's memorial. (Clay pieces for the children who died at the Dana-Faber Cancer Institute and Children's Hospital, Boston, MA). Ceramics Monthly May 1997 v45 n5 p22 W

Reflections

Be patient and kind to yourself.

My heart goes out to each of you reading this book that, like me, has lost a child. In talking with mothers and fathers it does not matter the age one's child dies or the age of the parent. We mourn the loss of our baby

I hope you found something between the covers to ease your pain.

Some days we are able to laugh and feel joy again – but other days we feel like a black cloud is hanging over us.

Remember.... You aren't crazy.

You are a grieving parent who is missing someone who should have still been in your life.

Mary Jane and Jeremy

I would be honored if you would like to email me with comments about the book or if you want to share your own story, you can reach me at griefgirl57@yahoo.com or visit my page at http://www.myspace.com/november_mourning

November Mourning

If you would be interested in participating in my survey please send responses to my email griefgirl57@yahoo.com.

- *What type of grief counseling or outside support did you receive?*

- *How has your family changed or dealt with the loss of your child?*

- *What are you doing now to help recover from the loss of your child?*

- *Where did you go for support?*

- *Who helped you the most with your grief?*

- *How would you like your child remembered?*

Reflections

About the Author

Mary Jane Cronin has extensive experience in bereavement counseling for individuals and groups. She has lectured on grief and bereavement and taught bereavement support skills to teenagers, incarcerated women, hospice patients and their families, as well as to volunteers, and fellow health care professionals.

Mary Jane earned her Bachelor's Degree in Human Development from Eckerd College in St Petersburg, Florida and her Master's Degree in Community Psychology from Springfield College in Tampa, Florida.

Providing counseling services in the Tampa Bay area of Florida since 2000 Ms. Cronin has been employed by The Hospice of the Florida Suncoast since 2004 as a Licensed Mental Health Counselor.

November Mourning